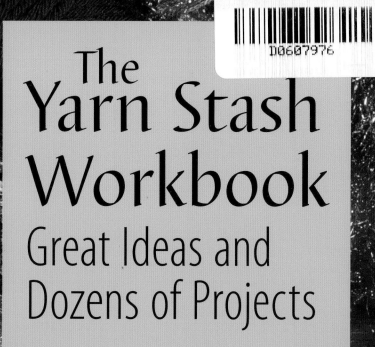

The Yarn Stash Workbook

Great Ideas and Dozens of Projects

LAURA MILITZER BRYANT

The Yarn Stash Workbook:
Great Ideas and Dozens of Projects
© 2006 by Laura Militzer Bryant

Martingale®
& COMPANY

Martingale & Company
20205 144th Avenue NE
Woodinville, WA 98072-8478 USA
www.martingale-pub.com

Credits

President .... Nancy J. Martin
CEO .... Daniel J. Martin
VP and General Manager .... Tom Wierzbicki
Publisher .... Jane Hamada
Editorial Director .... Mary V. Green
Managing Editor .... Tina Cook
Technical Editor .... Ursula Reikes
Copy Editor .... Durby Peterson
Design Director .... Stan Green
Illustrator .... Robin Strobel
Cover and Text Designer .... Stan Green
Photographer .... Brent Kane

Printed in China
11 10 09 08 07 06   8 7 6 5 4 3 2

Dedication

To my ever-patient and beloved husband, Matt

Acknowledgments

A lifetime of learning has gone into this book. I would like especially to thank my mom, Kay George, who taught me to knit and started me on this whole incredible fiber journey. Two of my professors at the University of Michigan School of Art and Design were of particular influence: Vincent Castagnacci, who taught me to see; and Sherri Smith, who taught me that all things are possible and pushed me to never give up, all the while sharing a great deal of knowledge concerning textiles. My friend and frequent collaborator, Barry Klein of Trendsetter Yarns, is always available for brainstorming and problem solving, and his willingness to share is treasured. The staff at Prism Yarns is ever supportive: Debbie, Di, Dragana, Jennifer, Lillie, Martha, Matt, and Will—thanks for being so patient. There would be no books without my talented sample knitters: Karen, Kay, Marge, Martha, Terry, and Ursula. The staff at Martingale—and particularly Ursula Reikes—deserve thanks for being, once again, a joy to work with and true collaborators in this endeavor. Thanks to you all.

Library of Congress Cataloging-in-Publication Data
Bryant, Laura Militzer.
    The yarn stash workbook : great ideas and dozens of projects / Laura Militzer Bryant.
        p. cm.
    ISBN 1-56477-614-X
    1. Knitting—Patterns. 2. Yarn. I. Title.
    TT820.B8723 2006
    746.43'2041—dc22
                                                        200528414

Mission Statement

Dedicated to providing quality products and service to inspire creativity.

CONTENTS

INTRODUCTION

Let's face it, knitters love yarn. We love to feel it, look at it, dream about it, possess it, and eventually knit it. Sometimes we love it more in the skein than when knit, but I hope this book will help make that happen less often.

Personally, I think knitters worry too much about their stashes. Who can complain about having bags of beautiful yarns to touch and dream about? After all, collectors exist for every type of item—coins, butterflies, art, stamps, golf clubs (familiar, anyone?), baseball cards—you name it, someone collects it. So, what's wrong with having a yarn collection? If it brings you pleasure, enjoy it rather than feel guilty about it!

Your stash can become part of your home decor: beautiful baskets or glass bowls filled with wild texture and color—what more could you ask for? Change the colors to suit your mood or the season. I have an antique coffee grinder in the corner of my dining room. My dear husband put raw white yarn in the top, spilling out, and finished skeins of hand-dyed yarn in the bottom drawer where the grounds once collected. He commented: "Well, Laura is really grinding out the yarn this week!" At Christmas, baskets are filled with red, green, and white yarns. And goodness knows, if you get confined to your house due to inclement weather (we have hurricanes; many of you have snowstorms), it's always good to know there is something you can work on.

In case you can't tell, I, too, am an inveterate yarn junkie, and my stash threatens to overtake my studio. Writing this book was great fun, because I had the chance to apply everything in it to my situation and that of several friends. Of course I used my own stash extensively, and since I own a yarn company, I'll admit to having a lot of Prism yarn in the stash. But I love all kinds of textiles, so you will find that I have used yarns from many different companies. Several friends contributed their stashes as well: my technical editor, Ursula; my sister, Karen; and my production assistant at Prism Yarns, Martha. Each one had fun letting me "have at" their stash. Each one gave me an idea of what they might like to have as a finished product, and many of the patterns grew out of their ideas. Several projects that I developed are shown in a variety of yarns so that you can see how adaptable a basic pattern can be. Most of all, we figured out how to use up a lot of those odds and ends we all have. Upon completing one wrap that used a skein each of six different yarns, Ursula's comment was: "Who knew all those yarns would look so great together?" Well, I guess I did, and my hope is that after reading this book, you, too, will have confidence in putting together colors and textures in unexpected ways.

IN THE BEGINNING: SORTING YOUR STASH

There are several things to consider regarding your stash. Quantities, yarn types, yarn weights, and colors will vary tremendously, and all have to be taken into account. Begin by setting aside any yarns of sufficient quantity for a whole project. These yarns can be sorted according to gauge, and suitable patterns found or created. Evaluate them for weight and type, and record that data. Carry a record with you on trips to your local yarn shop or bookstore; as you look at new pattern books, you'll know what you have at home that might work.

More problematic for most of us is the rest of the stash: sale yarns in odd amounts, leftover bits and pieces from other projects, yarns missing labels, and unusual or odd skeins that we just had to have because we loved them! If you're like me, you have all the above and more. The first thing to do is sort according to yarn weight. Although at one time yarns were referred to by names such as "fingering," "baby," "sport," "DK," "worsted," "bulky," and "chunky," those names best described smooth, plied classic yarns. The handknitting industry has come up with a new system for identifying yarn weight, one that takes into account the novelty textures available today.

YARN-WEIGHT SYMBOLS						
Yarn-Weight Symbol and Category Names	1 SUPER FINE	2 FINE	3 LIGHT	4 MEDIUM	5 BULKY	6 SUPER BULKY
Types of Yarn in Category	Sock, Fingering, Baby	Sport, Baby	DK, Light Worsted	Worsted, Afghan, Aran	Chunky, Craft, Rug	Bulky, Roving
Knit Gauge Ranges in Stockinette Stitch to 4"	27 to 32 sts	23 to 26 sts	21 to 24 sts	16 to 20 sts	12 to 15 sts	6 to 11 sts
Recommended Needle in US Size Range	1 to 3	3 to 5	5 to 7	7 to 9	9 to 11	11 and larger

Colors randomly juxtaposed

The same colors arranged by color weight

Although many older yarns, and some new ones, don't carry these designations, you can easily sort yarns into yarn weights by looking at the suggested gauge. For any yarns that are not labeled, make your best guess by comparing them to other yarns, or better yet, swatch them so that you really know. Notice that flat ribbon yarns tend to be in a lighter weight group than one would think from looking at the width of the ribbon. That's because most yarns are round, not flat, and the ribbons will roll when knit, causing them to be much narrower in a stitch than they are when laid flat. Since there is a range of suggested gauges instead of one set gauge for each weight, we can also consider subcategories; for example, slightly thinner size 5 versus thicker size 5 yarns. This is more important when substituting yarns for an entire project and less so when sorting yarns that can be used together.

Now, within each yarn-weight range, the yarns should be sorted by color. My approach has been formed by my art training; I studied color using the methods of Josef Albers, an important artist of the Bauhaus School who emigrated from Germany to the United States prior to World War II. He was less concerned with color wheels and schemes than with using our eyes to really see. While one does need to have a sense of the color wheel, as in being aware that yellow and blue make green, more important than slotting something into a scheme based on the wheel is learning to judge color weight. Albers referred to color weight rather than value because color weight takes into account such things as saturation and intensity, rather than merely the amount of black or white in a color. So instead of

light and dark colors, we refer to light and heavy colors. It's an odd quirk of the English language that the word light is the opposite of both dark and heavy.

When you look at any two colors, the lighter color will seem to advance while the heavier color recedes. It is as simple and as complex as that. Artists spend years training their eyes to detect fine nuances in weight between colors, but our purposes don't require anything that sophisticated. A simple understanding of light to heavy is all we need. Take a look at the photo at the top of page 6: a collection of every color under the sun. It is hard to make any visual sense of it. The lightest and the heaviest colors stick out noticeably, and the middle colors get lost. Very heavy shades tend to look generically dark, while the lightest colors lose their personalities and fade to neutral. All in all, it's a bit of a mishmash. I find it hard to imagine making any visual sense of this!

The bottom photo shows the same yarns arranged roughly from light to heavy color weights. Notice that highly saturated colors fit in next to duller ones. Our eye moves over the range smoothly; the colors are a nuanced wave, with few specific tones popping out. Subtle shades of pale colors are apparent. Deep tones take on richer hues. Notice that yellow is inherently light, so only the heaviest gold tones are in the middle areas and all other yellows are at the light end. Now we can evaluate and choose colors successfully.

Color Weight Affects Pattern

Let's look at stripes when different color weights are used:

A. The colors are as far apart as you can get—black and white. The stripes are very obvious and kinetic.

B. A rich, slightly multicolored red from the middle of the color-weight range is substituted for white, and although the stripes are still obvious, it is much easier to look at. We are very aware of the richness of the color.

C. Another multicolor from the same middle area of the color-weight scale is substituted for the black, and the effect is much less "striped" and more about the colors, which tend to brighten and intensify one another.

Here is another example, in a chevron stitch:

A. Two yarns are in two-row stripes. One color is from the heavy end of the scale, while the other is from the middle. The stripes are very distinct and graphic. The heavy color appears almost black.

B. The middle of the swatch replaces the middle color with a multicolor from the heavy end of the scale. The stripes are much less obvious and we have an awareness of rich color. The color weights are so similar that the striping is almost completely hidden.

C. A third, slightly lighter, multicolored yarn is added to the two colors in swatch B, and the stripes are worked in one row each. Some lighter notes are added and the stripes are visible but not overwhelming. The heaviest color actually shows up more, and it helps define the chevron.

> **These are the most important lessons one can learn about color in knitting:**
>
> • If you want to emphasize pattern, pick colors from different areas of the color-weight scale.
> • If you want to emphasize color, pick colors from the same area of the color-weight scale.

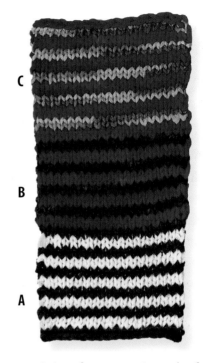

Bottom: Stripes from opposite ends of the scale (A)

Middle: Stripes from the heavy end and middle of the scale (B)

Top: Stripes from the middle of the scale (C)

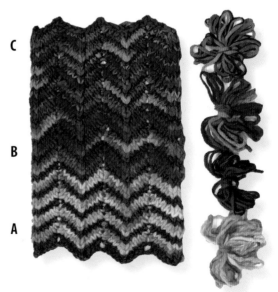

Bottom: Contrasting stripes from the middle and heavy end of the scale (A)

Middle: Two colors from the heavy end of the scale (B)

Top: A third, slightly lighter color added (C)

Pattern and Color Affect One Another

Let's look at the same colors as in the first swatch but knit in a different pattern stitch. The stitch is linen stitch, worked in two rows of each color. It produces a distinctly woven-looking, tweedy fabric.

A. The black and white combination is very kinetic.

B. The red and black combination is still tweedy, but much easier to look at and rich in color.

C. The two multicolors are magical, with stitches blending in some areas and popping out in others as the color weights shift subtly within the multicolors. The tweediness is much less obvious, and the colors enhance one another.

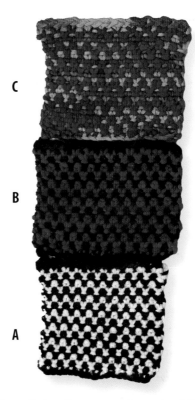

Bottom: Colors from opposite ends of the scale (A)
Middle: Colors from the heavy end and middle of the scale (B)
Top: Colors from the middle of the scale (C)

Why Bother?

Is it possible to get colors too close together? No, if what you want is a blending of colors (think Impressionist paintings), but yes, if what you want is to enhance pattern knitting. Look at this simple mosaic-boxes stitch. The outline color is the same from bottom to top, but the box color changes. The bottom is definitely a case of "Why bother?"— the colors are pleasant and blend together nicely, but they blend too well for the boxes to show. If you want to use these types of colors together, do simple stripes—much less work for the same result. Switching to a contrasting color allows the boxes to show up—much more worth the effort and easier to knit too!

Differing color weights enhance pattern; similar color weights enhance color.

Sorting by Yarn Type

After sorting by yarn weight and color weight, the last sorting to do is by yarn type. There are many yarn styles, and their different constructions affect how the yarn will behave, so it's useful to know something about them. Yarns may be the same gauge and yet produce fabrics with very different hands. Hand involves the total feel of a yarn, both in the skein as the yarn is being knit and in the final fabric—soft or crisp, limp or firm, thick or thin, spongy or stiff. Yarns of the same construction share certain characteristics, but sometimes fiber content has a greater effect on the hand or the way the yarn feels and behaves after it is knit. While there are no absolutes for selecting or substituting yarns, knowing something about their construction certainly does help.

Plied

Plied yarns are the most "normal" type of yarn, the kind many of us learned to knit with. They are typically smooth, have an obvious twist to them, and are made of thin strands that are run together to make a thicker yarn. Plied yarns may have thick and thin characteristics to give them a more homespun look. They generally have good resilience, even if made from nonelastic fibers such as cotton or rayon, because twisting builds some elasticity into the structure.

The plies can run side by side or be twisted. When plies are parallel, the yarn is more loosely constructed and has a rustic, homespun look; when plies are twisted, the yarn is stronger and smoother when knit. The plies themselves can be twisted loosely or tightly. The twists of the plies often run in the opposite direction of the twist of the final yarn, to cancel any overtwisting.

Bouclé

A bouclé yarn is characterized by a looped surface and is formed by the creation of small, medium, or large loops during the spinning process. The yarn is made by running a fiber through a spinning machine. At regular intervals the machine stops pulling the fiber, but the flow of yarn through the head of the spindle continues, creating a loop. The length of time that the pull is stopped determines loop size. To keep the loop in place, a support thread is wrapped around or chained into the yarn. Bouclés made from animal fibers are typically light and airy when knit. Rayon and cotton bouclés can become dense and heavy, and can be difficult to knit tightly enough for the fabric to maintain its shape. Because of this, they are best used in combination with other yarns, either in stripes or pattern stitches or worked purposely loose as in scarves or wraps.

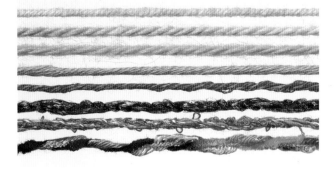

A range of plied yarns. Some are very smooth and others have more texture.

A range of bouclé yarns. Loops can be large or small, regular or random

Chained and Knitted

If you have ever made I-cord, you have made a knitted chain or tube. In the yarn industry, high-powered machines with up to 12 hooks or needles in a circle create chained or tubular yarns. The number of needles determines the thickness of the finished tube. Chained yarns are typically thin and appear round. We refer to larger and more tubular constructions as knitted tapes, because they flatten if there is no filler inside them. A chained yarn will run like pantyhose if the end is pulled. The end can be secured by knotting it or applying a small dab of clear nail polish or Fray Check. Chained yarns are often heavy and thick and have less yardage than plied yarns, but for fibers that tend to pill (become matted with little bits of fiber that ball up on the surface from abrasion), chaining is a great construction; the threads used to create a thicker yarn are themselves very thin. This allows the fiber ends to be securely captured, with little chance of escaping into pills.

A range of chained and knitted yarns. Wider tubes tend to flatten, while narrower chains stay round.

Brushed

Brushed yarns start as either a chained or bouclé yarn. The yarn then indeed goes through a brushing process. Like the tines of a dog's brush, metal teeth are set on a round cylinder and the yarns are then run over the teeth to brush up the base yarn. A chained brushed yarn is made in tubular fashion with a fiber that can be brushed. The strength of the chained yarn will hold up against the metal teeth pulling at it and will allow the brushed fiber to loft up, creating a hair. When the loops of a bouclé yarn are run up against the teeth, one end of the loop is broken free from the binder, creating a brushed effect. If you look at mohair closely, you will see a thick clump along the support thread that was the base of the loop before it was pulled loose. Brushed yarns produce a fuzzy, light and airy fabric, with the brushed hairs filling in space around the stitches. The fabric is generally very light-weight relative to the thickness of the stitches.

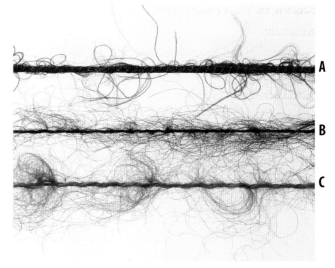

A range of brushed yarns on chained (A) or bouclé (B and C) bases

Chenille

Chenille is created on a circular spinning machine that has two heads. The narrow center head holds core fibers that are strong and twist at high speed. The outer head runs in a circular motion, injecting threads through the center fibers that get locked into place. At this point the yarn consists of loops that are captured at the center. The strand is run against extremely sharp razors, cutting the loops. The fast rate of speed that is used and the necessity of capturing the pile fibers securely often results in excess twist. Chenille is steamed after it is created to release the twist, yet some twist remains. As a result, chenille can loop or "worm" after it is knit. The strands relax and they want to shed their extra twist, resulting in loops of yarn appearing on the surface of the knitted piece. The solution is to knit chenille extremely tightly so that the stitches have nowhere to move. Stitches such as linen stitch, which becomes quite tight due to all the slipped stitches, can help stabilize chenille. Some chenille yarns with a wool core can be felted to lock the stitches in place without affecting the velvety pile.

A range of chenille yarns. Thicker yarns have longer loops injected and then cut. The cores are all thin.

Woven

Woven yarns, or ribbons, are woven on very narrow looms or made on a modified weaving loom. The base of the modified machine is similar to a knitting machine: a flat bed with very small needles lined up. The width of the ribbons depends on the number of needles engaged. Each needle produces a small chain, through which horizontal threads are inserted. Pull the horizontal, or weft, thread out of the end of a ribbon and you will see the vertical fibers, or warp, set free. When worked on larger needles, woven ribbon will remain wide and flatter, and will produce a lighter weight, draped fabric. With smaller needles, the ribbon will fold and create a crimped look, becoming denser, stiffer, and heavier. The density of the weaving affects the feel of the ribbon: some are more loosely woven and behave more like yarn, while others are very tightly woven and stay much crisper and more ribbonlike.

A range of woven ribbons. The ribbon at bottom was made on a modified weaving loom. The others were woven on a standard loom.

Nubs and Slubs

A nub is created when a yarn is twisted and pulled through rollers on a twisting machine. When the pulling stops but the twisting continues, a nub occurs. Depending on the length of time the pulling has been stopped and how slowly the pulling begins again, the nub can be big and full or narrow and long. Nub yarns are also called slub or bump yarns. When knit, the nubs tend to go to the purl side, making garter and reverse stockinette good stitch choices. Nub yarns require a smaller needle because they have a tendency to knit too loosely, creating a flimsy fabric.

A range of nub yarns showing size and frequency variations

Component Yarns

Yarns that are generally too thin to knit alone are considered components, because they are often mixed with another yarn to produce a desired weight. Despite their exuberant texture, component yarns are built on a thread-thin base. An industrial weaving loom that has hundreds of small hooks on a flat bed is used to make them. Each hook creates a chain, and the desired texture is created by a high-speed spindle that shoots back and forth through the chain, injecting small components that are locked in place.

Eyelash-type yarns have long hairs attached to the base chain. The eyelash yarns produce a furry surface that can be airy or dense, depending on the frequency of the lashes. It is not necessary to pull all the hairs through to the outside while working, although some knitters do. Lashes and flags will tend to fill in the open spaces around each stitch, so often a larger needle than one would think can be used. The texture will be most noticeable on the purl side.

Other components can look like railroad tracks, pom-poms or balls, or paperlike flags. The base chain may have other plies twisted around it or have metallic spikes added—the variations are almost endless! Technology for fiber manipulation has grown

phenomenally in the past two decades, and yarn designers invent new and different ways to create components on a daily basis.

Many of these textures are better combined with other yarns, either by holding a strand together with the other yarn or by knitting alternating rows of the yarns, because the thin base produces somewhat flimsy fabric. However, they can be successfully worked as sheer fabric on larger needles for scarves, wraps, and tunics meant to be worn over dresses or camisoles. In the marketplace, you can find yarns that consist of components that have been plied with other strands to make them more user-friendly, but many of the components are sold alone so that you can become your own yarn designer.

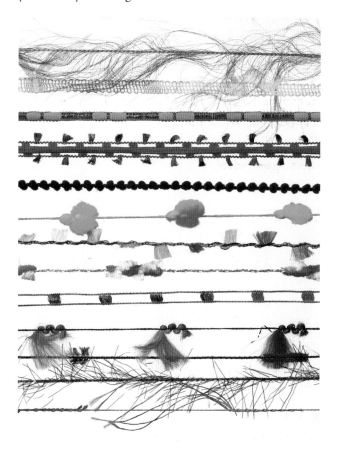

A range of component yarns. Some are thin and should be worked with other yarns, while others have been combined at the factory and will work on their own.

THE RIGHT YARN FOR THE RIGHT PROJECT

We knitters are an enterprising lot. Rarely do we knit a garment exactly as shown or with the yarn specified by the pattern. Most often we fall in love with a yarn first, and then we look for a pattern in the same gauge. Sometimes the results are less than we had hoped for, because our finished garment neither looks as good as the model nor shows off the yarn as we had envisioned. There are many factors to consider besides gauge. While matching gauges will produce a garment that fits, the hand of the knitted fabric and the type of yarn selected will affect the look and feel of the finished project. When working with stash yarns, it is especially important to consider all the variables, because good information about the yarn is often lacking: the yarn may have no label, or you may be combining a number of yarns in the same project. While I know some of you will shudder at the thought, you really must swatch! It's the only way to learn about the yarn you are contemplating using, and it will save time, effort, and tears later on.

Gauge

The first step to developing a project is creating a swatch. If the yarn is labeled, there should be a suggested needle size and recommended gauge. If there is no label, make your best guess according to the thickness of the yarn and the type, and by comparing it to other yarns that are labeled. Cast on at least 4" worth of stitches—more is better, and keep in mind that you may be working in a stitch with a pattern multiple.

For example, if the suggested gauge is 3½ sts = 1" on a size 10½ needle, cast on at least 14 stitches (3½ x 4"), casting on more as needed to get to a correct multiple plus edge stitches if there is a pattern stitch. Work in stockinette stitch or the pattern stitch for at least 2". Stop to feel the swatch and look at the stitches. Evaluate the fabric: Are the stitches too loose or tight? Are they even? Is the hand too soft or stiff, too limp or thick? Make the necessary needle adjustments, up or down, to correct what you don't like. If the fabric is much too loose, go down several needle sizes; if too tight, go up. If fine tuning is all that is required, change one needle size and continue

until you have at least 3" of knitting whose hand you like. Bind off your swatch.

Lightly block the swatch with steam. Determine the gauge by measuring across the entire swatch, from edge to edge, and then divide the number of stitches by that measurement. Repeat for the rows worked. If there is a fraction involved, round up to the nearest half stitch or row per inch. Record the needle size and stitches and rows per inch, and keep it with the project. Now you can select a pattern that calls for the same gauge.

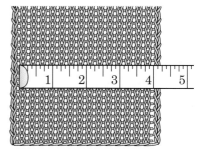

There are other considerations as a project plan is developed. Once the gauge is determined, consider

A variety of swatches tells a lot about the yarn and how it will behave.

Curl along the stockinette edge (left) and seed stitch border folding over (right)

the hand of the swatch and its suitability for various uses. A soft, draped fabric might not make great outerwear, while a purse needs something with body to keep its shape and hold up to heavy use. How the swatch behaves will also tell us much about the finishing of a garment: what type of borders, trims, and edgings will work.

Have any of the following happened to you?

- Your newly knitted cardigan is in stockinette stitch, and the front bands refuse to lie flat, always folding in unless the garment is buttoned. Or worse, you have used the purl side out and the bands fold to the outside.
- The summery cotton you substituted for wool in a ribbed pattern looks flat and lifeless.
- Your stockinette stitch scarf curls at the edges, and even if you add a seed stitch border, the border itself folds over.
- You want a rolled finish at the hem and neckline, but the yarn you chose refuses to roll.

All of these occurrences result from the natural tendency of stockinette stitch to roll, coupled with the resilience and elasticity of the yarn. Stockinette stitch will curl toward the purl side along the side (selvage) edge (which is why scarves roll) and toward the knitted side along the cast-on or bound-off edge (which is why rolled collars and hems work).

Curl along the top and bottom edges

In garments, the selvage edge curl is controlled by seaming at the sides and by borders of rib, garter, or other flat stitches at the bottom, top, and front edges (of a cardigan). Scarves, shawls, and throws have edges that are more difficult to control.

The more elasticity a yarn has, the more it will roll. Elasticity is the amount of stretch that bounces back when a strand of yarn is held under tension and then released. To check a yarn, grab a ruler. Measure 12" of yarn with no tension, and then pull on the strand and check the measurement. Many novelty yarns, cottons, and rayon will move less than an inch or so—very little elasticity. Woven tapes are the most solid, moving only about ¼". Most plied wools, chained yarns, and many nylons will move a lot—up to 2" or more, or 15% to 20%! Flatter and less stretchy yarns are not as prone to rolling and will make a flatter knitted fabric. Yarns with more stretch will produce fabric with more natural curl.

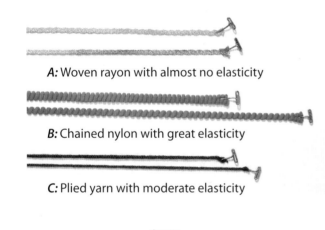

A: Woven rayon with almost no elasticity

B: Chained nylon with great elasticity

C: Plied yarn with moderate elasticity

The other factor that affects rolling is the tightness of the knit. Smaller needles produce tighter stitches with more tendency to curl. One reason that many novelty yarns lie so flat is that they are almost impossible to knit tightly, especially bouclé. Mohair, which is often knit loosely, tends to lie flat. To encourage rolled edges, make sure that they are worked on a needle several sizes smaller than that used for the body. I have used rolled edges successfully even on a cotton crepe, which knits quite flat, by working the edge on a very small needle.

The same moderately elastic yarn is flat (left) when knit loosely and curled when knit tightly (right).

Cotton with negligible elasticity is knit very tightly at the bottom to encourage roll; the looser top is flat.

Left: Knitted nylon with great elasticity has lots of roll.

Right: Plied rayon/cotton with little elasticity is very flat.

Yarn choice also affects the texture of a pattern stitch. The large-scale rib shown below was worked both in very stretchy nylon/rayon chainette and in flat woven rayon with no stretch at all. The deep rib is quite dimensional in the chainette, and much flatter in the woven.

Left: Flat woven ribbon produces a flattened rib.
Right: Chainette with good elasticity produces a rib with much more dimension.

So, in addition to gauge, here are several factors to consider when selecting a project for your yarn:

- The elasticity of the yarn—how much stretch is in the original and the substitute?

- The construction details of the garment—is it a cardigan to be left open? A casual sweater with rolled edges? A highly textured stitch pattern? A draped wrap?

- More elastic yarn produces greater roll in stockinette stitch and more relief in textured stitches.

- Less elasticity produces less roll and flatter texture.

- To keep a highly elastic yarn flat when knitted, select a stitch other than stockinette. There are many stitches that will work. Anything that combines knits and purls on the same side will lie flat: garter (even though you only knit, it is in essence a row of knit alternated with a row of purl on the same surface), rib, seed, basket weave, and on and on. Your scarf or cardigan edge won't roll if it's worked in one of these stitches!

In conclusion, swatch and think about the proposed purpose of the project. Careful selection of appropriate yarn will ensure success.

DESIGN TRICKS

Sometimes there is almost enough yarn for a whole project. Or, we think there is, but we're just not sure. Then our bodies grow a little and there definitely isn't enough anymore! This happens to everyone, but there are clever ways to use the yarn you do have so that it doesn't look like you skimped or ran out. I consider design to be visual problem solving, and having less than enough material is definitely a problem. Often the search for a practical solution results in a more successfully designed garment, especially when working with novelty yarns. Yarns with highly textured, forward personalities can overwhelm the wearer if used throughout an entire garment. One solution is to find a compatible yarn that is a wallflower—one that will disappear into the background, allowing your important yarn to shine. Then select a pattern, be it stripes or a pattern stitch that uses two yarns. Over the years I have developed a repertoire of tricks that seem to work in endless ways. This chapter will cover some of my favorites. I hope you find them useful too. If nothing else, perhaps they will inspire you to look at your own favorite stitch patterns and ways of working in a new light.

A variety of ways to use two or more yarns in combination

Borders and Trims

If you know you are going to run short, there are lots of strategies for adding other yarns. But what happens if you were sure (or hopeful) that there would be sufficient yarn—and there isn't? My first hint is to always check how much yarn was used after completing one body piece. Figure that a front and back will take the same quantity, and long sleeves will take half of the total front and back quantity again. Short sleeves will take about a third of the front and back combined, and cap sleeves about a quarter.

Then there is finishing—hopefully there is already a border at the bottom, and you won't need a great deal to finish the neck (if there are fronts to finish, they will of course take more) but you do need to take that into account. Discovering after completion of one piece that there is insufficient yarn allows a much better chance of developing a design that won't look like you ran out. Or, read the rest of this chapter, tear back what has been knit, and then redesign the garment. If you do get to the end and there isn't enough, consider using a contrasting yarn for trim, as we did for the Convertible Cardigan on page 116. This will be much less noticeable on something that is multicolored, where you can repeat some of the colors. Notice that the front bands were tied visually to the rest of the garment by adding a row of crochet in the trim yarn to the bottom edges. If borders have already been worked in the main color, they can be taken off and reworked in the contrasting yarn to tie the garment together. The Painter's Palette Pullover on page 102 is another example; here, a solid color unifies the whole. The point is that thinking about solutions before your back is against the wall is far preferable to making last-minute decisions—but in either case, help is at hand!

Borders can help stretch yarn quantities and provide design interest.

One-Row Stripes

I love combining different textures and colors. Often we see stripes worked in two or more even rows, and I have found that this frequently concentrates too much of one color or texture, particularly when combining different yarn weights. One-row stripes are visually effective. Because they are only one row thick, they tend to mix optically (like an Impressionist painting) and appear like allover color instead of standing out as stripes, especially if elements from the same part of the color-weight scale are used. It is the perfect way to use different textures or colors, because there is never enough concentration of any one thing to make a strong statement.

To make one-row stripes:

Cast on with A.

Drop A, attach B, and work across.

Drop B, attach C, and work across.

Drop C, and A, is waiting for you.

You can work on either straight or circular needles, and in garter, stockinette, or other textured pattern stitches. It is easy to keep your place—always begin at the side where there are two yarns available to work, and don't use the yarn just worked. To keep the yarns from twisting, place one on either side of you and one between your legs. Notice that turning in one direction twists the strands, but turning the other way keeps them straight. Sometimes you need to pass one strand over the needle to the front or back to keep it in place.

A variety of swatches in
one-row stripes

Fibonacci Stripes

Leonardo Fibonacci lived in Italy from the mid-twelfth through mid-thirteenth centuries. He was essentially responsible for introducing Arabic numbers (which we use today, as opposed to Roman numerals) to the Western world. What he is best known for, though, is the discovery of certain numerical relationships that are found frequently in nature. These numbers occur in a sequence that reads thus: 1, 1, 2, 3, 5, 8, 13, 21, 34, 55, and so on. Each number is formed by adding the current number to the previous number: $1 + 1 = 2 + 1 = 3 + 2 = 5 + 3 = 8$, and so on.

These numbers describe naturally occurring patterns, such as the genealogy of a male bee, the branching of plants and flower buds, and the whorls of a nautilus shell. Also, the number of petals in any given flower from many different species is often a Fibonacci number: 3 (irises, lilies); 5 (buttercups); 8 (delphiniums); 13 (ragwort, some marigolds); 21 (asters and some marigolds); 34, 55, and 89 (different types of daisies). Once you get past the first few digits, each pair of numbers has a ratio (1:1.6) that is known as the golden mean and describes the golden rectangle. If one side of a golden rectangle is taken as value 1, the other side will always be 1.6 times that dimension. Golden rectangles have been found throughout art and architectural history, and were well known to early civilizations. It seems an interesting coincidence that Fibonacci numbers describe that ratio.

So, enough academics! What do Fibonacci numbers have to do with knitting? As did the artists and architects of millennia past, modern designers often use Fibonacci numbers in their work. The numbers are useful for designing proportions and subdividing space. For knitters, they provide an ideal sequence for stripes. The following set of swatches, here and on page 22, shows a variety of ways that Fibonacci numbers can be used and how they differ from predictable two-row stripes.

Plain stripes in two rows of each color

Left: The same colors in a Fibonacci sequence:

- 1 row with A, 2 rows with B, 3 rows with A; 1 row with B, 2 rows with A, 3 rows with B

Right: The same colors in a different sequence:

- 1 row with A, 1 row with B, 2 rows with A, 3 rows with B

Left: 3 colors in a repeat of 3 numbers:

- 1 row with A, 2 rows with B, 3 rows with C.

Right: The same 3 colors in a repeat of 4 numbers:

- 1 row with A, 1 row with B, 2 rows with C, 3 rows with A;

- 1 row with B, 1 row with C, 2 rows with A, 3 rows with B;

- 1 row with C, 1 row with A, 2 rows with B, 3 rows with C;

- 1 row with A, 1 row with B, 2 rows with C, 3 rows with A, etc.

This looks much more complex due to the changing of both the color and the number of rows.

Interesting, isn't it? With the same colors, the sequences have different visual impact, because varying quantities of color are used in each one. This is a great way to play around with stripes that aren't boring and predictable.

STRATEGIES FOR ALMOST ENOUGH

Often we find we're short by just a little bit of yarn. While it's tempting to plunge ahead and take our chances, a much safer alternative is to develop a design plan that adds another yarn. Adding stripes is an obvious answer and easy to figure out. Once you have chosen a pattern, either from this book or another, find the materials list. Multiply the number of skeins of suggested yarn required by the yardage given. This is the total number of yards needed to make the garment. Multiply the yardage from the main yarn (the one there isn't quite enough of) by the number of skeins you have. Subtract this from the total yardage, and you know how much yarn must be added to make the project work. Now for the fun part: to figure out how many rows of each yarn should be worked for a repeated stripe pattern, simply look at the yardages.

Let's walk through the math for the Almost-Enough Striped Tee on page 94, using the medium size as an example.

5 skeins x 95 yards = 475 yards
2 skeins x 58 yards = 116 yards
Total = 591 yards (Round up to 600 for ease of calculation.)

If you had a substitute yarn that was 80 yards per skein, you would need 7½ skeins (or 8, because we always round up to whole skeins). But there are only 6 skeins, leaving a shortage of 120 yards (600 needed–480 in hand = 120 short). After finding 120 yards of compatible yarn, how often must we stripe to make the yarns come out equally? There are several ways to do a quick estimate. The easiest in this case, because there are only 2 yarns, is to look at the accent yarn as a percentage of the main yarn: 480 divided by 120 is 4, so for every 4 rows of main color, you will work 1 row of contrasting color. The easiest way to do that is to work 8 rows of main color and 2 rows of contrasting color, which happens to be the same as needed for the yarns used in our model, even though the total yardages are a bit different. If there were only 5 skeins of the 80-yard yarn (400 yards), you would need 200 yards of accent. 400 divided by 200 = 2.

So, for every 2 rows of main color, you would work 1 row of contrasting color. That translates easily to 4 rows of main color and 2 rows of contrasting color. Of course the math won't always work out so neatly, but remember to round up yardage requirements, and the quantities should be sufficient.

If there are several colors you would like to use together in stripes, make sure there is more than enough total yardage to make the appropriate size, and be conservative in your estimate—you don't want to run out! Total up the yards for each color. For example:

A: 285 yards
B: 360 yards
C: 480 yards
D: 125 yards
E: 195 yards

A quick and easy way to do stripes is to look at the numeral indicating the hundred multiple, ignoring the tens and ones. Work stripes thus: 2 rows with A, 3 rows with B, 4 rows with C, 1 row with D, 1 row with E. This sequence is easily worked on circular needles, sliding back and forth as needed to pick the appropriate yarn. Or, double the numbers for even rows: 4 rows with A, 6 rows with B, 8 rows with C,

2 rows with D, 2 rows with E. If the yarns are used in these proportions, there will be more left of all but D, but there won't be extravagant amounts remaining.

Six rows of main color are accented with two rows of contrasting color.

Linen and Half Linen Stitch

Linen stitch is often called fabric stitch because it resembles woven fabric. It is useful for mixing up different yarns and colors, because they intermingle on every row. Every other stitch is slipped every row while the working yarn is carried on the right side. Either two rows of A, two rows of B, or one row each of A, B, and C work nicely to balance disparate yarns. Each yarn will be needed in equal amounts, so each yarn can be roughly a half or a third of what you need for an entire project. My preferred pattern is shown below:

Over an even number of stitches:

Row 1 (RS): *K1, sl 1 wyif, rep from * across.
Row 2: *P1, sl 1 wyib, rep from * across.

Notice that when you slip the stitch, the working yarn is carried across the right side, making a small horizontal bar. A stitch is worked and then the carried yarn is "woven" across the next stitch, which is why it looks so much like fabric—in essence it is a combination of knitting and weaving. Always slip

stitches as if to purl so that they are in the correct position for the next row. If working on uneven stitches, simply add an always-worked selvage stitch.

Over an uneven number of stitches:

Row 1 (RS): K1, *sl 1 wyif, rep from * to last st, K1.
Row 2: P2, *sl 1 wyib, P1, rep from * across.

You will find that linen stitch is very firm and flat, making it great for edgings and for reversible items (the back is attractive, also). Most of the time a needle two sizes larger than recommended for a given yarn is needed to keep the fabric from becoming too boardlike. This stitch is one of the few ways chenille can be worked tightly enough, so work it on the recommended needle size. Linen stitch will also control any over-twisting in yarn (see page 76): even though it is a form of stockinette, the stitches that are carried across the right side are stabilizers, canceling the tendency to pull off square.

Half linen stitch is a variation that works almost as well as linen stitch at blending colors and textures. In half linen, all stitches on the wrong side rows are worked.

Over an even number of stitches:

Row 1 (RS): *K1, sl 1 wyif, rep from * across.
Row 2: Purl.
Row 3: K2, *sl 1 wyif, K1, rep from * across.
Row 4: Purl.

A variety of linen and half linen swatches

Half linen stitch does not pack as densely as linen stitch, so a needle only one size larger may be required to get a nice hand. This variation will not control chenille, because the purled row will not work tightly enough. Linen or half linen stitch can be applied to any pattern, as long as the gauge is the same and you like the hand of the fabric.

Pattern Stitches

Small-scale pattern stitches are also great for combining yarns when you don't have enough of any one thing for a project. There are myriad stitch dictionaries out there—it's definitely worth the investment to have one or two in your library. Look for mosaics and two or three color patterns that have small repeats. Work a gauge swatch, and as long as your gauge matches, you can apply a pattern stitch to any existing pattern.

A variety of pattern stitches using two yarns

Patterns using two rows of each yarn in a balanced amount, such as many mosaic stitches, will use equal amounts of each yarn. A stitch with a strong main color accented with smaller amounts of contrast might use two-thirds main color and one-third contrasting color. As always, don't cut it too short—better to have some left over, to become the inspiration for another project, than to run short.

Mohair Is Our Friend

Mohair is the great equalizer! Light, fluffy, airy, and luxurious, it can pump up a gauge while adding softness and warmth. Mohair is generally found in two varieties: kid and regular. Fine, soft kid comes from baby Angora goats. It is usually a light-weight yarn, one that would knit on its own at about 6 stitches per inch. Regular mohair, from adult Angora goats, has hairs that are longer and coarser than kid, although still soft and airy. Regular mohair often knits at about 3½ stitches per inch, making it a bulky-weight yarn. Either one, when held as a strand along with other yarns, will stabilize slinky yarns, add warmth to cotton or rayon, hide imperfections in a yarn that might snag, and add bulk without extra weight.

Kid mohair is more desirable for pullovers that are worn next to the skin, while regular mohair is great for outerwear. However you choose to blend mohair, it can stretch a short yardage and turn a component into a full-blown yarn.

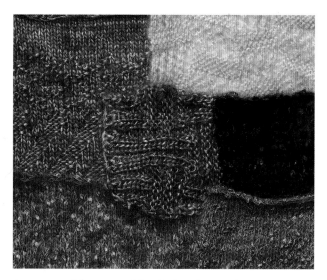

A variety of thin yarns blended with mohair

These tricks and more have been explored in the patterns that follow. Hopefully they will spur you, my valued readers, on to efforts of your own. Feel free to apply any trick to any pattern—take some risks, try it your way. I'll close with my favorite saying: "You don't get *wow* by doing the expected!"

Small amounts of yarn suggest scarves. There are many scarf patterns floating around, but this section features three of my favorite approaches. A good scarf will be flexible, will have nice drape, and should not roll on the edges. Stockinette is not a particularly good choice for scarves, both because it has a distinct right and wrong side, and because no matter what border

Scarves, of Course

you attach, most yarns will roll. Every time I visit an online knitting bulletin board, another new knitter is asking how to keep her scarf from rolling! The easy answer is to not use stockinette. Additionally, scarf patterns are adaptable to a wide range of yarns because gauge and finished size are not critical. If you wish your scarf to be an exact measurement, make a gauge swatch so that you can determine how many stitches you must cast on.

Accent Scarves

Sometimes you just want a simple accent for a special outfit. It might be too hot for a sweater, or your silk blouse cries out for some knitted attention. These jewelry scarves are the answer. Not too bulky, not too big, and definitely meant for beauty and not warmth, they allow you to wear your knitting on every occasion. The best thing is that they use very little yarn. Working on the diagonal keeps the knitting interesting and produces a gracefully tapered bottom edge. I like mine tied in a loose four-in-hand knot, just like a man's tie, midway down instead of close to the neck. If the yarn is very soft, tying each end in a knot adds weight for a nice drape. With fringe or without, these are good to go with any look!

Size

Approx 6" x 70"

Materials

Approx 200 yds *total* of fine- or light-weight
    novelty yarns (2) (3)
Size 10 needles

We Used:

3 skeins of Sunshine from Prism Yarns (1 oz; 65 yds),
    color Freesia* (3) (shown on page 29)
*As an alternative, you might also try 3 skeins of Biwa
    from Prism Yarns (1 oz; 68 yds), color Senegal (3)
    shown on previous page at far right. Or, 2 skeins
    of Dazzle from Prism Yarns (1 oz; 116 yds), color
    Sagebrush (3) shown on previous page in middle
    photo.*

Scarf

- CO 24 sts.
- Work in garter st and K1f&b at beg and K2tog at end of every RS row. Mark selvage with a pin: when pin is at beg of row, it is a shaping row. Knit all WS rows even.
- Work to end of yarn, saving some for fringe if desired. BO all sts.
- Attach fringe to short edges, trim evenly.

Bulky Variation

The same basic instructions can be used to make a scarf with thicker yarns. Since the stitches are bigger, you will need fewer stitches and less yardage.

Size

Approx 6" x 70"

Materials

Approx 100 to 150 yds *total* of medium- or bulky-weight novelty yarns (4) (5)
Size 13 needles

We Used:

2 skeins of Super Dazzle from Prism Yarns (1 oz; 90 yds), color Terra Cotta (3) shown on previous page at far left.

Scarf

CO 18 sts and work as for scarf at left.

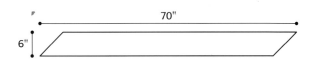

OPENWORK SCARF—OR WRAP?

Openwork scarves use the simple stitch of "YO, K2tog" on every row. This produces a lovely open and airy scarf with exceptional drape. It requires less yardage than one would expect, making it perfect for those wonderful balls we pick up on sale or that remain from another project. If you're more comfortable working "YO, ssk," it makes no difference to the appearance of the scarf.

The openwork stitch also allows you to use a wide range of yarn sizes. Anything from fine to a bulky- or super-bulky-weight yarn will work. The thicker the yarn, the less open the stitch will be. You can also use larger and larger needles as the yarn size increases. If you have different colors of the same yarn, or just three different yarns, this is a great place to use one-row stripes. You can also hold several thin strands together, such as adding an eyelash to a fine-weight yarn. And if you don't want to work the pattern stitch, garter is great too! Use a needle size larger than recommended to get better drape and make the yarns go farther. However, realize that the openwork stitch is more stable than loose garter stitch, and less likely to snag.

Don't forget, gauge and size are not critical for these pieces. Make a gauge swatch if you want an exact size.

Small scarf: A small scarf uses the least amount of yarn and is a nice accent piece. These are long enough to tie or wrap around your neck.

Large scarf: Thicker yarns and more stitches make a more generous scarf—a bit wider and longer. We're talking about drama here.

Wrap: Even more stitches produce a piece that can be scrunched around the neck like a scarf, or draped over the shoulder as a wrap. Who doesn't like flexibility?

Here are basic guidelines for different sizes of scarves and yarn weights worked in the openwork pattern.

	SMALL SCARF	LARGE SCARF	WRAP
Approx size	7" x 60"	9" x 70"	18" x 80"
Approx yardage	150 yds	275 yds	450 yds
Yarn weight	Fine, light, or medium (2) (3) (4)	Medium or bulky (4) (5)	Medium or bulky (4) (5)
Needle size	11*	11*	11*
Approx gauge to 4"	10 sts	10 sts	10 sts
Number of sts to CO	18 sts	24 sts	42 sts

If you're using a very bulky yarn, go up to a size 13 or 15 needle. Your scarf will automatically get larger, so use the small-scarf pattern numbers. By the same token, if you're using a fine-weight yarn, go to a size 10 needle and use a larger number of stitches.

Openwork scarves
Top left and right: Large scarf in Fern, small scarf: 3-yarn variation.
Bottom left and right: Small scarf in Dover, wrap in Pebbles.

Openwork Pattern

(Even number of sts)
Every row: K1, *YO, K2tog, rep from * to last st, K1.

Small Scarf in Dover

(Shown at bottom left on page 31)
Pretty pastels in an interesting novelty yarn create a ladylike accent scarf.

We used:

1 skein of Dover from Prism Yarns (2 oz; 150 yds), color Tea Rose 4

Size 11 needles

Scarf

CO 18 sts and work openwork patt to approx 60". BO all sts.

Small Scarf: 3-Yarn Variation

(Shown at top right on page 31)
If you only have single skeins, pick 3 and use 1-row stripes as described on page 20.

We used:

A—1 skein of Surf from Prism Yarns (2 oz; 56 yds), color Ginger 5

B—1 skein of Luna from Prism Yarns (1 oz; 58 yds), color Tea Rose 4

C—1 skein of Super Dazzle from Prism Yarns (1 oz; 80 yds), color Periwinkles 4

Size 11 needles

Scarf

- With A, CO 18 sts.
- Work 1 row stripes as described on page 31. Work as for small scarf in Dover at left, BO when first yarn runs out.

Large Scarf in Fern

(Shown at top left on page 31)
Although the texture of this yarn hides the openwork stitch, a large scarf can be achieved because the stitch pattern uses less yarn than garter stitch. The larger yarn is worked on bigger needles, so use the cast-on numbers for the small scarf.

We used:

2 skeins of Fern from Prism Yarns (2 oz; 45 yds), color Tumbleweed 5

Size 13 needles

Scarf

CO 18 sts and work openwork patt to approx 70". BO all sts.

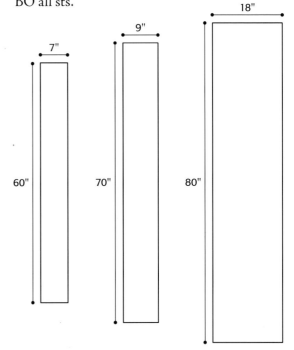

Wrap in Pebbles

We used:

(Shown at bottom right on page 31)

3 skeins of Pebbles from Prism Yarns (2 oz; 123 yds),
color Granite

Size 11 needles

Wrap

CO 42 sts and work openwork patt to approx 80".
BO all sts.

Small Scarf in Ritratto

(Shown at right)

Fine mohair flecked with a touch of metallic creates a
lovely drapable scarf. This would look great wrapped
or tied as shown. Ritratto is a finer yarn and to
approximate the small scarf size, we dropped down in
needle size and increased the cast on to the large scarf
numbers. This results in a slightly smaller gauge.

Size

Approx 6" x 72"

We used:

1 skein of Ritratto from Stacy Charles
(50 g; 198 yds), color 46

Size 10 needles

Gauge

16 sts = 4" in patt

Scarf

CO 24 sts and work openwork patt to approx 72".
BO all sts.

MULTIYARN WRAP OR SCARF

Here is a fun wrap that will work with many different yarns. I like to have at least five different textures, and if each averages about 80 to 90 yards per yarn, there will be enough for a generous wrap. It is knit very openly on a large needle, so gauge is not critical. The ends are tapered for added interest, and the fringe is made as each row is knit. The loosely knit fabric is very flexible, and if worn as a scarf, it falls in lovely, generous folds around the neck. For a wrap, hold along one long edge and shake to make the width grow larger. Set the wrap comfortably on your shoulders, with one long edge hanging down the front and at about knee height. Grasp the other long edge, which is the outside edge of the other side, and bring it over your other shoulder. The front will fall in a flat fold that doesn't add bulk and the wrap is long enough to sit on your shoulders.

This is a great use for odds and ends, and you will love having one in every color combination imaginable. I wear mine often in Florida, where even in the heat of the summer you must always have something to cover your shoulders in overly air-conditioned restaurants and theaters.

Size

Approx 15" x 80" to 100" (Size is measured along edge and depends on how loosely the wrap is knit. The 15" will lengthen to approx 20" if shaken to wear over the shoulders.)

Materials

Approx 450 yds of yarns in assorted textures and weights ranging from fine to bulky

Size 13 needles*

Size 15 needles*

Optional trim: Approx 200 yds of a smooth yarn; size H crochet hook

If you know that you are a tight knitter, use size 15 and 17 needles instead.

NOTE: Cast-on and bound-off stitches are made with a larger needle to ensure that the edges are as loose as the knitting; otherwise, the edges pull up while the middle sags. If you're using size 17 needles, which are really big, cast on over two size 13 needles. Or, if you prefer, you can choose to use an e-wrap (backward-loop) cast on instead of casting on or binding off over two needles. Begin with a slipknot on the needle. Put your right index finger under the yarn, pointing toward you. Turn your finger to point away from you, making a loop around your finger. Insert the tip of the needle through the loop in the same direction as your finger. Remove finger and draw the yarn snug, forming a stitch. Repeat for required stitches.

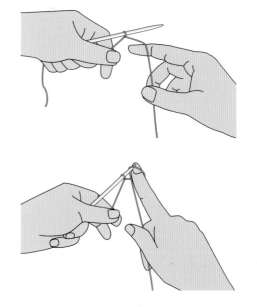

Version 1

Wrap or Scarf

Read all directions before beg.

- CO 150 sts with larger needle, or over 2 needles held tog.

- Change to smaller needle and work in garter st, working 1 row of each yarn in random order. At beg of each row, cut old yarn leaving a tail of about 8" and tie new yarn to old, snugging knot up to edge of knitting. This will become fringe. AT SAME TIME work shaping as follows: On all RS rows, K2tog at beg of row. On all WS rows, inc 1 st at beg of row. Place a safety pin close to beg of row on RS—if pin is at beg of row, it is a dec row; if pin is at other end, it is an inc row. You may have more yardage of some yarns, so work rows of those yarns more often.

- Leave enough yarn to BO, and use larger needle for BO.

Finishing

- Cut any rem yarns approx 16" long, and add to ends as additional fringe.

- If desired, use smooth yarn to work 1 row sc and 1 row rsc along long edges.

TIP: If any of the yarns you have selected tend to unravel, tie a very tight knot at the tip of the cut end, or apply a spot of Fray Check to secure the end.

We Used:

VERSION 1

1 skein of *each* of the following:

Kos from Missoni (116 yds)

Rococo from Prism Yarns (72 yds)

Brazza from Missoni (93 yds)

Rialto from Stacy Charles (65 yds)

2 skeins of Astra Missoni (110 yds)

VERSION 2

1 skein of *each* of the following:

Vision from Trendsetter Yarns (66 yds)

Bon Bon from Prism Yarns (88 yds)

Cleo from Prism Yarns (82 yds)

Sunshine from Prism Yarns (68 yds)

Trillino from Prism Yarns (85 yds)

Dazzle from Prism Yarns (116 yds)

2 skeins of Touch Me from Muench Yarns (61 yds) used for trim only

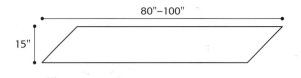

Version 2

Loose fitting over-garments are easy and fun to make, and are a good choice for unknown and mixed yarns. The generous sizing allows differing gauges to be used together because there is no need for tightly controlled measurements. These are great projects for less-experienced knitters—you'll learn new techniques, become more comfortable with larger amounts of knitting, and wind up with a beautiful and useful finished garment. Toppers can range from traditional ponchos to wilder ones,

Toppers

from ruana and serape styles to capelets. All are marked by minimal shaping and can be worn over normal street clothing. Made with classic or novelty yarns, these pieces will serve you for a lifetime. Go wild with your yarn choice—now is the perfect time to experiment with yarn combinations!

UPDATED RUANA

Novelty yarns intrigue us with their exuberant texture and often confound us when it comes to using them effectively. A simple garment such as this ruana is a great solution. The sizing is not critical, so it can be adapted over a number of different gauge types, and the shape is simple, so difficult yarns are easier to cope with. It's worked in garter stitch so that all the edges lie flat. Garter stitch also helps showcase the yarns, because many novelty effects are pushed to the purl side. A very unusual or dear yarn can be shown to great advantage by using it for trim alone or by striping it sparingly against plainer yarns. The loose style of the ruana is reminiscent of a shawl or wrap, but because it has side seams and armholes, it sits firmly on your shoulders and doesn't have to be grasped to stay put.

Ribbons Ruana

Lots of ribbons and textured yarns create a playful yet dressy ruana. Cutting and tying each yarn after one row creates a "self fringe" at the bottom edge.

Size

Approx 30" wide x 30" long, including fringe and measured on the body

Materials

Approx 1000 yds *total* of ribbon and novelty yarns in the following weights: light, medium, bulky, and super-bulky (3) (4) (5) (6)

Size 13 needles, or size to obtain gauge

Size 15 needles (for CO and BO)

Size J crochet hook

We Used:

1 skein of Rococo from Prism Yarns (3 oz; 72 yds), color Aruba (4)

1 skein of Fern from Prism Yarns (2 oz; 45 yds), color Tropicana (5)

1 skein of Charmeuse from Prism Yarns (1¾ oz; 72 yds), color Deep Purple (4)

1 skein of ½" Ribbon from Prism Yarns (3½ oz; 95 yds), color Aruba (6)

1 skein of Bubbles from Prism Yarns (2 oz; 68 yds), color Rio (4)

1 skein of Flash* from Prism Yarns (2 oz; 125 yds), color Fantasia (3)

3 skeins of Checkmate from Trendsetter Yarns (50 g; 70 yds), color 1036 (5)

3 skeins of Dolcino from Trendsetter Yarns (50 g; 99 yds), color 10 (3)

Flash must be knotted at the end each time it is cut to stop fraying.

Gauge

8 sts and 24 rows = 4" in garter st on smaller needles working 1 row of each yarn

Hold swatch vertically when measuring to allow for downward stretch.

NOTE: This garment and Showcase Ruana at right are worked in one piece from side to side, and the weight of the ribbon causes the garment to grow substantially in length and also to narrow. For example, the actual knitting will be approximately 43" wide from side to side and 48" long. This will narrow to approximately 30" wide from side to side and grow to approximately 60" long when the garment is worn. We have taken that into consideration when writing the patterns.

Ruana

- With larger needle and a smooth ribbon, CO 94 sts using an e-wrap (see page 34) or cable CO.

- Change immediately to smaller needle, cut yarn, leaving an 8" tail, and tie another yarn to this tail as if you were knotting fringe (which you are; the tails become the fringe).

- In garter st, work 1 row of each yarn, cutting and tying a new yarn each row. Use yarns you have more of more often, and yarns you have less of less often. Alternate thicknesses and textures randomly.

- Work as established to 20", then divide for front: With larger needle, BO 47 sts. Change back to smaller needle and work for 3" more, working each yarn for 2 rows and cutting and tying at bottom edge only.

- With larger needle, CO 47 sts, change to smaller needle and work 2nd side to 20". Knit 1 more row with larger needle, then BO with larger needle.

Finishing

- Fold piece in half RS tog with fringed edges aligned. With crochet hook, slip st seams together along side edges from bottom up for about 12", leaving approx 12" opening.

- With any smooth ribbon and crochet hook, work 1 row rsc around front and neck edges, and around armhole openings. Trim fringe evenly.

Showcase Ruana

I purchased a stunning handspun mohair bouclé yarn some time ago. There were only 38 yards in the hank, so I knew the application would be limited. I enjoyed fondling that skein for years, and then I decided it had to be used. An adaptation of the Ribbons Ruana suggested itself: a soft blend of kid mohair and shiny rayon in three different colors used in one-row stripes became the body; then the mohair curls became the focal point at the edge. I eliminated the fringe for a more tailored look and because I wanted to draw attention to the mohair curls. A simplified crochet edge really showed this yarn to its best advantage.

Size

Approx 30" wide x 30" long when measured on the body

Materials

A, B, C—Approx 800 yds *total* of bulky-weight yarn 🔢5

D—Approx 40 yds of super-bulky novelty trim 🔢6

Size 13 needles or size needed to obtain gauge

Size 15 needles

Size J crochet hook

We Used:

BODY

3 skeins *each* of Kid Slique from Prism Yarns
(2 oz; 88 yds) in colors Alpine (A), Brass (B), and
Harvest (C)

TRIM

Approx 40 yds Handspun Mohair Curls from Pastora
the Color Lady (D)

Gauge

10 sts and 20 rows = 4" in garter st on smaller needles
with A, B, and C

Ruana

- With larger needles, CO 110 sts.

- Change to smaller needles and work as for
Ribbons Ruana, but instead of cutting and tying
yarn at end of each row, carry yarns loosely along
edge. We used 3 colors, A, B, C, in 1-row stripes
as described on page 20.

Finishing

- Fold piece in half and sew side seams for approx
12", leaving approx 12" for armhole opening.

- With A and crochet hook, work 1 rnd sc around
bottom, front, and neck edges, do not cut. Attach
B and work 1 row sc along bottom edge, cut B.
Attach C and work 1 row sc along bottom edge,
cut C. With A, work 1 row sc along bottom edge.

- With D, attach yarn at lower-right front, and with
WS facing, work *ch 2, skip 1 st, slip st in next st*
across bottom; work 1 slip st in corner, then rep
from * to * for front and neck. Fasten off. Rep last
rnd at armholes.

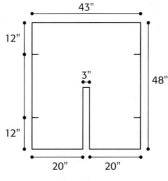

Knitted measurements

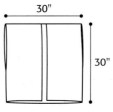

**Measurements
when worn**

Playful Ponchos

Poncho, poncho, who has that poncho? We all do—or if we don't have it, we want it! Not the bright orange acrylic monstrosities from the sixties, the new ponchos have great yarns, great shapes, and new details. They can go from black-tie events to football games and everything in between. Ponchos are easier to wear than a wrap or a shawl, because there are no open tails, and they stay put on your shoulders. Make them in bulky, warm yarns for outerwear; in silky, metallic yarns for dressy times; or in a variety of fun textures for a real fashion statement. It's easy to customize your poncho with yarn selection.

Our variations include a multiple-yarn version, both in classic yarns and crazy textures, and a more sedate three-yarn version. It's hard to believe they're all from the same set of instructions! Instead of fringe at the bottom, one multiple-yarn poncho uses all the ends created when joining new colors by tying those tails together to make fringe that marches down the side seam—all as you work. The three-yarn version has no ends except when joining a new ball, so a decorative crochet edge defines the side seams. I have found that these shaped ponchos fall better on the body when worked in two pieces with a side seam for structure, but if you really wanted, you could eliminate the seams and work in the round by casting on twice the number of stitches. If you work circularly, garter stitch must be worked by knitting one round, purling one round.

Novelty Poncho with Bottom Fringe

Select a large variety of ribbons and other playful yarns. There will be unequal amounts of yardage for each yarn. Use the yarns with more yardage more often, and those with less yardage less often. The front and back do not have to match exactly. The goal is to create a lovely, blended fabric—not to showcase each individual yarn or to make distinct stripes. Extra yarn gets cut and attached to the bottom edge for fringe.

Sizes

Small (Medium, Large)
See diagram for measurements.

NOTE: The weight of the yarn causes the poncho to grow in length and to narrow in width. We have taken that into account when writing the pattern.

Materials

Body: Approx 900 (1000, 1100) yds *total* of assorted light-, medium-, or bulky-weight yarns (3) (4) (5)

Trim: Approx 120 yds of medium-weight ribbon or chenille (4)

Size 11 needles or size required to obtain gauge

Size H crochet hook

We Used:

1 skein *each* of the following:

Coconut from Trendsetter Yarns (50 g; 65 yds), color 126

Aquarius from Trendsetter Yarns (50 g; 96 yds), color 810

Trillino from Prism Yarns (2 oz; 85 yds), color Meadow

Dazzle from Prism Yarns (1 oz; 116 yds), color Wisteria

Bon Bon from Prism Yarns (2 oz; 88 yds), color Periwinkles

Bon Bon from Prism Yarns, color Wisteria

Cleo from Prism Yarns (1½ oz; 62 yds), color Meadow

Dover from Prism Yarns (2 oz; 150 yds), color Tumbleweed

Rococo from Prism Yarns (3 oz; 72 yds), color Sierra

2 skeins *each* of the following:

Sunshine from Prism Yarns (1 oz; 65 yds), color Sierra

Touch Me from Muench Yarns (50 g; 62 yds) for trim, color 3626

Gauge

12 sts = 4" in garter st

Poncho

- With smooth yarn, CO 30 (40, 48) sts.
- **Next row:** K14 (19, 23), pm, K2, pm, K14 (19, 23).
- ***Next row:** Knit to marker, sm, P2, sm, knit to end.
- Work as follows:

   Row 1: Knit to 1 st before marker, K1f&b, sm, K2, sm, K1f&b, knit to end.

   Row 2: Knit to marker, sm, P2, sm, knit to end.

   Rep rows 1 and 2 until piece measures 22 (24, 25)" from neck to bottom point or desired length. BO all sts loosely.

- Rep for other side. The 2 pieces do not have to match*.

Finishing

- With WS tog, trim yarn, and crochet hook, work 1 row sc and 1 row rsc along each side seam. Work 1 rnd sc and 1 rnd rsc around neck edge.

TIP: Because the ponchos are knit with a relatively loose gauge for the weight of the yarn, you can crochet an edge with one crochet stitch in each knit stitch. Normally, this would be too crowded and would create a wavy edge. To make a neat reverse-crochet edge, drop down one hook size and work one reverse stitch in each single crochet stitch.

- Cut fringe from remaining yarns and trim, and add to bottom edge. If using slippery yarn such as Touch Me for fringe, pull strand fully through edge, fold strand over, even ends, and tie overhand knot.

Three-Yarn Striped Poncho

Here is a more traditional poncho. Select three yarns of varying color and texture. They do not have to be the same weight, but they should be within a two-size range (for example, two yarns that are bulky and one that is medium, or two bulky and one super-bulky. Label them A, B, C. Work one-row stripes as described on page 20. This version does not have fringe along the side seam.

Sizes

Small (Medium, Large)
See diagram for measurements.

NOTE: The weight of the yarn causes the poncho to grow in length and to narrow in width. We have taken that into account when writing the pattern.

Materials

Approx 700 (750, 800) yds *total* of bulky-weight and super-bulky-weight yarns

Size 13 needles or size required to obtain gauge

Size J crochet hook

We Used:

4 skeins of Savvy from Trendsetter Yarns (100 g; 60 yds), color 26

3 skeins of Mogador from Muench Yarns (100 g; 99 yds), color 105

5 skeins of Grain from Prism Yarns (2 oz; 65 yds), color Embers (1 skein is used for edging)

Gauge

10 sts = 4" in garter st

Poncho

Refer to page 20 for working one-row stripes.

- CO 24 (30, 40) sts.

- K11 (14, 19), pm, K2, pm, K11 (14, 19).

- Work from * to * as for Novelty Poncho with Bottom Fringe on page 46.

Finishing

With WS tog, trim yarn, and crochet hook, work 1 row sc and 1 row rsc along each side seam. Work 1 rnd sc and 1 rnd rsc around bottom and neck edges.

Multiyarn Poncho with Side Fringe

Martha, my production assistant, made this one from her stash. She calls it the "Frances Poncho" because it was made while waiting for, during, and in the aftermath of hurricane Frances, which pounded Florida over Labor Day weekend in 2004.

Leave a tail approx 8" long each time you change yarn, which should be every row if you want fringed sides. Tie the new yarn to the old, and these tails become fringe once the poncho is finished. Or, make random stripes of more rows per yarn and use the extra to fringe the bottom edge.

Sizes

Small (Medium, Large)
See diagram for measurements.

NOTE: The weight of the yarn causes the poncho to grow in length and to narrow in width. We have taken that into account when writing the pattern.

Materials

Approx 1200 (1350, 1500) yds *total* of light-weight yarn (3)

Size 9 needles or size required to obtain gauge

Size G crochet hook

We Used:

1 skein *each* of La Laine from Brunswick (100 g; 260 yds), colors 6245 Sage and 6220 Rice Paper (3)

1 skein of La Laine Bouclé from Brunswick (100 g; 245 yds), color 4620 Rice Paper (3)

3 skeins of Arbor from Brunswick (100 g; 245 yds), color 7704 Southwest Ombre (3)

1 skein *each* of Evergreen from Classic Elite Yarns (100 g; 226 yds), colors Oatmeal and Brown (3)

Gauge

15 sts = 4" in garter st

Ponchos

- CO 40 (50, 60) sts.
- K19 (24, 29) sts, pm, K2, pm, K19 (24, 29) sts.
- Work from * to * as for Novelty Poncho with Bottom Fringe on page 46.

Finishing

With WS tog and fringe aligned and loose on RS, use crochet hook to work slip st seam along side, underneath fringe knots. Work 1 rnd sc and 1 rnd rsc around bottom and neck edges.

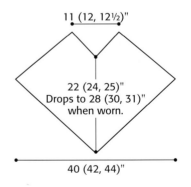

11 (12, 12½)"

22 (24, 25)"
Drops to 28 (30, 31)"
when worn.

40 (42, 44)"

OPENWORK CAPELET

I find myself attracted to (and collecting) lots of shiny yarns, often with hints of metallic. Although my lifestyle isn't such that I often wear dressy clothes, I do love them. A beautiful gold ribbon in my stash called out to be used in some kind of topper that could go over different types of outfits. Usually when collecting yarn I wind up with a bag of 10 skeins, which often limits what can be made. As noted in the openwork scarves, "K2tog, YO" combinations provide a lovely open fabric that doesn't use as much yardage as other knit structures.

This capelet is a stunner with unusual shaping. Use any soft, slippery ribbon or yarn, ranging from light-weight to bulky-weight. The thicker the yarn, the less open the stitch will be. The combination of "ssk" and "k2tog" skews the "middle" a little off center, providing a nice asymmetry, which is enhanced by the lettuce-type ruffled edging.

Size

See diagram for measurements.

NOTE: The weight of the yarn causes the capelet to grow in length and to narrow in width. We have taken that into account when writing the pattern.

Materials

6 skeins of Verikeri from Muench Yarns (50 g; 113 yds), color 4102

Size 11 circular needle (24)" or size required to obtain gauge

Size F crochet hook

8 stitch markers

Gauge

7 sts = 4" in openwork patt

16 sts and 24 rows = 4" in St st (in case you have difficulty in determining gauge in patt)

NOTE: It's difficult to take an accurate gauge on knitting as open as this. Take the swatch off of the needle and, without stretching in any direction, measure. If you know that you're a tight knitter, go up to a size 13 needle automatically. Because this yarn is rayon with a knitted tape construction that is worked so openly, the fabric of the capelet will stretch both widthwise and lengthwise, depending on the pressures put on it. The instructions will be the same for any size, but if you want a larger size, get another ball or two of yarn, and simply make the length longer. The openwork will stretch widthwise, making the cape shorter. The gauge is also provided in stockinette stitch, which may be helpful.

Capelet

- CO 66 sts. Knit 2 rows.
- **Next row:** K2, *pm, K13, K1f&b, pm, K2, pm, K1f&b, K13, pm*, K3, rep from * to *, end K1.
- Knit 1 row.

- **Next row:** K2, sm, *K14, K1f&b, sm, K2, sm, K1f&b, K14, sm*, K3, sm, rep from * to *, end K1.

NOTES:

- Increases are placed on both sides of the middle front and back, every row. They are made with a "K1f&b." Two sets of markers in different colors help to keep track of front/back versus sides. Use one color for the center front and back, and the other color for the sides. There are no increases at the sides.

- While knitting this capelet, I found that by wrapping the yarn in the opposite direction during the "ssk" sections, the stitches were facing correctly for the next round without my having to reverse them. When you reach an "ssk" section, instead of wrapping counterclockwise, try wrapping clockwise, including the yarn over. While it may seem awkward at first, the ease of working the next round makes up for it, and it's surprising how quickly one can adapt to the different wrap direction.

- Join to beg circular knitting and work rnds as follows:

  Rnd 1: K2, sm, *(YO, K2tog) to 2 sts before marker, K1, K1f&b, sm, K2, sm, K1f&b, (ssk, YO) to 1 st before marker, K1, sm*, K3, sm, rep from * to *, end K1.

  Rnd 2: K2, sm, *(YO, K2tog) to 1 st before marker, K1f&b, sm, K2, sm, K1f&b, K1, (ssk, YO) to 1 st before marker, K1, sm, K3, sm*, rep from * to *, end, K1.

Rep rnds 1 and 2 until piece measures approx 28"; you should have used 5 skeins. It takes almost an entire skein to do ruffled bottom edge and crocheted top edge.

> **TIP:** You can identify which round you're on by counting the stitches between markers: round 1 will have even numbers, and round 2 will have odd numbers.

- Work ruffled edge as follows:

  Next rnd: K1f&b in each st around.

  Next rnd: K1f&b in each st around. BO all sts.

Finishing

- Sew first 3 rows tog at top edge.
- With crochet hook, work 1 rnd sc and 1 rnd rsc around neck edge.

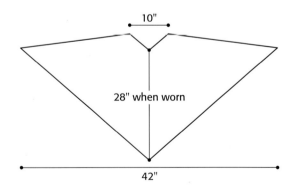

10"

28" when worn

42"

Little bits of yarn are perfect for funky, fun accessories. Hats and purses are two of my favorite vehicles for getting wild and crazy with knitting. This is a place to really be creative and free those inhibitions—after all, these are small projects and they won't take that much time to make. You might learn something about color, pattern stitch, or yarn combinations that

Accessories

had never occurred to you before and that can be used in a bigger project. Sometimes giving oneself permission to experiment is a great catharsis— no rules, no right or wrong, just knit it!

A good basic hat pattern can work for anything from a close-fitting watch cap to a medium or long tailed stocking cap. The difference is simply the rate of decrease: for a watch cap it happens quickly, while a stocking cap spreads the decreases out over a longer distance. Hats, particularly stocking caps, seem to lend themselves to stripes— which also happen to be a great way to use up odds and ends of yarn! Although it is easy to work this type of cap in the round, I prefer to work anything that has stripes flat and seam it later. Stripes worked in the round show a jump where the colors shift. If worked flat, the stripes can be seamed to one another exactly. If you wish to make any of these caps in the round, simply subtract two stitches from the total (these are allowed for seaming) and work on a short circular needle. You will need to move to double-pointed needles or two circular needles when the stitches are too few to fit comfortably any longer. I used an "invisible" cast-on method, which produces a very elastic, rolled edge that works perfectly for hats.

BASIC STOCKING CAP

I had several skeins of pretty teal wool and lots of odds and ends of angora and cashmere. They were fairly compatible in weight, so I plunged in. One-row stripes are a great way to integrate different yarns, so that suggested a striped cap. There was enough solid-colored cashmere for the rib band and enough multicolored cashmere for use in the body. I tied the angora together once in every row, staggering the knots and allowing them to sit on the outside as an extra fun touch. The little knots became part of the design—instead of burying the tails, they float on the surface as added decoration. Of course, you could weave them on the inside if you prefer a cleaner look. I added I-cord tails to one hat, and a thick tassel to the other.

Sizes

Small (child) [Medium (women), Large (men)]

Approx circumference: 20 (22, 24)", slightly stretched
    and above rib band

Materials

Approx 250 (300, 350) yds *total* of medium-weight
    yarn (4)

Size 5 needles*

Size 7 needles or size required to obtain gauge*

*Use circular or double-pointed needles if you prefer to
work in the round.*

We Used:

For each stocking cap:

A—1 skein of Montana from GGH (50 g; 70 yds),
    color 25 Teal (4)

B—Approx 1 skein of Angora from Prism Yarns
    (1 oz; 90 yds) in assorted colors (4)

C—Approx 1 skein of Cashmere from Prism Yarns
    (3½ oz; 164 yds) in assorted colors (4)

Gauge

16 sts and 22 rows – 4" in St st on larger needles,
    alternating 1 row of each yarn

Cap

- With smaller needles and scrap yarn, CO 36
  (38, 42) sts using the invisible CO method as
  follows: Change to cuff yarn and K1f&b in each st
  except last 1—73 (77, 85) sts.

  Next row: K1, *sl 1 wyif, K1, rep from * across.

  Next row: Sl 1 wyif, *K1, sl 1 wyif, rep from *
  across.

  Rep last 2 rows once more, and then remove scrap
  yarn by carefully cutting it every few inches and
  gently pulling it out.

NOTE: To work in the round, join now and pm.

- Work K1, P1 ribbing for 3", or for 6" if you want a cuff that folds back.

- Change to larger needles and St st and knit 1 row, inc 9 (13, 13) sts evenly spaced across—82 (90, 98) sts.

- Beg alternating 1 row each A, B, C as described on page 20. This works for knitting flat. If knitting in the round, simply wrap new strand around 2 nonworking strands.

- Work St st for 3", then beg shaping:

- **Dec row:** Dec 8 sts evenly spaced across next row as follows: K1, *K2tog, K8 (9, 10), rep from * to last st, K1. Work dec row every 8th row 4 times, working 1 less st between dec every time (total 40 sts dec)—42 (50, 58) sts rem and approx 6" of St st worked.

- Beg dec every 2", and dec 6 sts evenly spaced 3 times—24 (32, 40) sts. Dec 4 (5, 6) sts evenly spaced every 2" three times—12 (17, 22) sts. Dec 3 (4, 7) sts evenly spaced at next 2"—9 (13, 15) sts. Work 2" more, then dec 0 (4, 6) sts—9 sts. To finish without tails, thread tail onto tapestry needle and pull tail through rem 9 sts and gather them up. For optional tails, see below. St st section is approx 22" long.

Finishing

- If you worked hat back and forth, sew seam with mattress st (see page 122).

- **Optional tails:** Work I-cord as follows: Knit first 3 sts on needle with color A, sl those sts back to left needle, then carry yarn tightly across back and K3. Leave other 6 sts on needle for later. Cont to work same 3 sts in I-cord as established for 12". BO 3 sts. With color B, work next 3 sts in same manner, and last 3 sts with color C. Use yarn tail to close end of cord. You can let cords hang free or braid them.

- **Optional tassel:** Wrap leftover yarn around a 3"- to 4"-wide piece of cardboard. The more wraps used, the fuller the tassel will be, but use at least 80–100 strands for medium-weight yarns. Tie a 12" scrap of double yarn tightly around 1 side of group. Cut opposite end. Smooth ends tog, away from middle tie. Wrap another piece of yarn tightly around tassel, about 1" from tie. Tie off and bury these ends in middle of tassel. Trim ends evenly. Use tie yarn to attach to cap. See illustration on page 69.

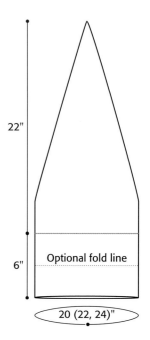

22"

6"   Optional fold line

20 (22, 24)"

WATCH CAP

The same basic stocking cap pattern made this close-fitting watch cap that's finished with a pom-pom on top. A single multicolored yarn was used for a more masculine look. The hand-dyed yarn provides enough interest that I didn't need to knit stripes. I stuck with cashmere because it is luxurious and feels so good on the forehead, but there are a lot of beautiful yarns that would work equally well. Only one skein is required, so although it is a bit of a splurge, it's a nice treat for someone special.

Size

Small (child) [Medium (women), Large (men)]
Approx circumference: 20 (22, 24)"

Materials

1 skein of Cashmere from Prism Yarns
   (3½ oz; 164 yds), color Smoke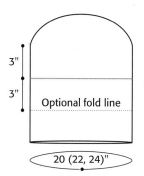

Size 5 needles

Size 7 needles or size required to obtain gauge

Gauge

16 sts and 22 rows = 4" in St st on larger needles

Cap

- CO and work band and initial part of head as for stocking cap.

- Work dec EOR instead of every 8th row, and cont as established with 1 less st between each dec to last 8 sts. Thread tail through sts and pull tight, then sew seam and attach pom-pom to center.

Finishing

Pom-pom: Wrap yarn around a 2" to 3" piece of cardboard, about 200 wraps. Tie very tightly with double strand of yarn; then cut other end and allow strands to bloom around tie.

3"

3" Optional fold line

20 (22, 24)"

CAP WITH EARFLAPS

Here's a fun cap the kids will love. Slip-stitched pinstriping is used in the body of the cap, while two-row garter-stitch stripes create the earflaps, giving a nice play of vertical versus horizontal stripes. The edges are trimmed with I-cord for visual definition and a crisp finish. Casting on with scrap yarn allows the open stitches to be used for both the ear flaps and the I-cord edging, and short-row shaping at the peak is hidden in the I-cord bind off. Knit this one in the round, because the pinstriping works beautifully and invisibly.

Size

Approx circumference: 22", not stretched

Materials

MC—Approx 100 yds of medium-weight yarn (4)

CC—Approx 100 yds of medium-weight yarn (4)

Size 9 circular needle (20") or size required to obtain gauge

Size 10½ circular needle (20") or size required to obtain gauge

Size J crochet hook

Stitch markers

We Used:

MC—1 skein of Kashmir from Trendsetter Yarns (50 g; 90 yds), color Black (4)

CC—1 skein of Kashmir from Prism Yarns (2 oz; 102 yds), color Tapestry (4)

Gauge

18 sts and 38 rows = 4" in garter st on smaller needles

18 sts and 40 rows = 4" in pinstripe patt on larger needles

Pinstripe Pattern in the Round

Rnd 1: With CC, K1, sl 1 wyib.

Rnd 2: With MC, sl 1 wyib, K1.

Rep rnds 1 and 2.

Cap

- With scrap yarn and crochet hook, ch 100. With MC and larger needle, pick up 1 st in each chain through the back loop of the chain st. Join, pm, and beg pinstripe patt. Work for 6", ending with completed rnd 1.

- **Shape peak:** Place a 2nd marker between sts 50 and 51.

   Rnd 1: *K2tog, work pinstripe patt to marker, sm, rep from *.

   Rnd 2: *Sl 1, ssk, work pinstripe patt to marker, sm, rep from *.

   Rep rnds 1 and 2 for 25 more rnds, ending with completed rnd 1—46 sts.

- Join 2 sides of hat, BO sts, and create an I-cord trim at same time as follows: Pull cable of needle out at marker in middle—2 sides of hat will line up along each needle tip. With smaller needle and MC, CO 2 sts, sl these 2 sts to 1 needle alongside cap. With 2 larger needle tips aligned and parallel,

*K1, sl 1 kwise (these are 2 MC sts just CO), sl 1 kwise from front needle, sl 1 kwise from back needle, sl all 3 sts back to left needle and knit all 3 sts tog, sl 2 sts back to left needle pulling yarn tightly across back, and rep from *. Cont until 2 sts rem, then BO I-cord as you finish last sts.

- **Earflaps:** Release scrap yarn and place all sts on smaller needle, placing a marker at center back. Attach MC and work 3 rnds garter st as follows: Purl 1 rnd, knit 1 rnd, purl 1 rnd. Attach MC in 10th st from marker, and work across 22 sts. Work garter st on these 22 sts, alternating 2 rows of MC with 2 rows of CC, for 18 rows.

- **Shape flaps:** Dec 1 st each edge every 4th row 3 times. Dec 1 st each edge EOR 2 times. Dec 1 st each edge every row 4 times—4 sts rem. Next row: K1, K2tog, K1—3 sts rem. With CC, work 18" to 20" I-cord tie on 3 sts as for stocking cap. Rep for other flap on opposite side.

Finishing

Attach CC to center back. Knit 1 rnd, and AT SAME TIME, PU 18 sts along each side of each ear flap (36 sts per flap), pushing tie to front and working behind it. CO 2 sts and work I-cord BO around entire hat as follows: *K1, sl 1 kwise, sl 1 kwise, sl those 2 back to left-hand needle and k2tog tbl, sl 2 sts back to left-hand needle, rep from *. Fasten off.

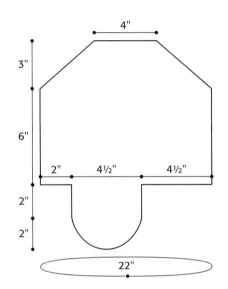

MITERED PURSE

Sometimes we run across an unusual yarn with great visual beauty and skein appeal, but once it has been knit, it doesn't meet our expectations. I had a nylon yarn caged in metallic that was very pretty, but tended to work up tightly and was a bit coarse. That immediately suggested a purse to me, because knitted purses often suffer from lack of structure and can be too flimsy to really use. Indeed, by working garter stitch on a smaller-than-recommended needle, I made my little evening purse firm enough to work without a lining, with stitches tight enough that things don't poke through easily. A trip to my trimmings stash produced a beautiful jet bead that I added along the edge of the flap. A garter-stitch gusset along the sides and bottom provided a bit of shaping instead of a completely flat envelope. Three strands of I-cord were braided for a stable, strong strap. The intriguing mitered shape would look good in a variety of fabrics—leftover recycled silk from the pillows shown on page 75 would be a nice choice for a more casual purse.

Size

Approx 4" x 8"

Materials

Approx 250 yds *total* (126 yds each of 2 colors, A and B) of medium-weight yarns (4)

Size 6 needles

51 beads

4 yds of strong beading thread

Size F crochet hook

Stitch markers

We Used:

2 skeins *each* of Lunette from Prism Yarns (1 oz; 63 yds) in the following colors:

 A—Smoke (4)
 B—Fog (4)

Flap

- String 51 beads on beading thread.

- With A, CO 56 sts. K28, pm, K28. Knit 1 row.

- Change to B and beading thread and holding both strands tog, work as follows:

  Row 1: Ssk, *sl bead to front, knit next st*, rep from * to * to 2 sts before marker, K2tog, sl bead to front, sm, ssk, rep from * to * to last 2 sts, K2tog, turn.

  Row 2: Knit 1 row. Leave beading thread attached for stabilizing beads later.

  Row 3: Ssk, knit to 2 sts before marker, K2tog, sm, ssk, knit to last 2 sts, K2tog, turn.

  Row 4: Knit.

  Rep rows 3 and 4, alternating 2 rows of A with 2 rows of B. When 4 sts rem, ssk, K2tog, psso to BO.

Back

- With A, CO 20 sts, PU 40 sts along top of flap, turn and using cable CO method, CO 20 sts. Knit 1 row.

- Change to B and set up shaping: K18, K2tog, pm, ssk, K38, K2tog, pm, ssk, K18. Knit 1 row.

- With A, *knit to within 2 sts of marker, K2tog, sm, ssk*, rep from * to *. Knit 1 row.

- Cont as established, alternating 2 rows A and 2 rows B, until 4 sts rem. BO all sts as above.

Front

- With A, CO 80 sts. K20, pm, K40, pm, K20. Knit 1 row.

- Change to B and work as for back.

Gusset

- Attach B to point between flap and back. PU 20 sts along side of back, 40 sts along bottom edge, and 20 sts along other side. Knit 1 row. Alternate 2 rows of A and B for a total of 10 rows, ending with color B.

- To join pieces, place front and back with RS tog, front in front and live sts of gusset on needle, with needle point in left hand. *Insert right needle into first st of front, then through first st on needle, wrap and pull through both pieces, rep from *, then BO first st. Rep for each st around until front and back are joined.

Finishing

- With crochet hook and B, work 1 rnd rsc around entire top and flap edge.

- With A, PU 3 sts along top of gusset, leaving room for 6 more sts. Work I-cord for approx 30", then place on holder. Rep with B for middle 3 sts. Rep with A for next 3 sts. Braid the 3 strands firmly. Graft to other side gusset.

- To stabilize beads, thread excess beading thread on needle and run through all beads to align them. Take a stitch in fabric of purse, and rep in other direction. Fasten off.

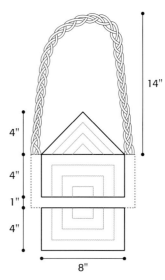

Sometimes our environment craves a bit of knitting just as our bodies do. There is nothing like snuggling up in a knitted throw, showing off our skills on decorative toss pillows, or crafting a touchable teddy. Instead of sitting folded in a drawer, these knitted pieces work 24 hours a day at looking good. They are great gifts, too, and if you can make them from stash yarns, all the better. My employees

Home Decor

and a group of friends have taken to making community baby blankets for new arrivals—I supply the yarn and get it going, then everyone takes a turn stitching on it. What a treasure for the new parents—every stitch is filled with love!

BLENDED THROW

An abundance of lush texture adds up to luxury. This throw is made with a base yarn that is carried throughout, with additional strands added and changed as you work. By starting at one corner and working on the bias, you can make the throw as large as your supply of base yarn will allow—when half is gone, it's time to decrease. Sort the textured yarns before beginning, both according to color and yarn size. Our base yarn was bulky-weight, and we used textured yarns from light-weight through bulky-weight, with a few super-bulky-weight: three strands of light-weight, or a light-weight and a medium-weight held together, or a single strand of bulky or super-bulky. The exact gauge doesn't matter too much, because you will change yarns often enough to even out the differences.

Size

Approx 56" x 72"

Materials

MC—Approx 1000 yds *total* of bulky-weight yarn (5)

CC—Approx 1000 yds *total* of assorted blending textures in the following yarn weights: light, medium, bulky, and super-bulky (3) (4) (5) (6)

Trim: Approx 500 yds *total* of assorted medium-weight yarns (4)

Size 17 needles (use 19 if you are a tight knitter) or size required to obtain gauge

Size J crochet hook

NOTE: If the main yarn is bulky-weight and the blending yarns are smaller sizes, take into account that you will need multiple strands of those yarns as follows: one strand of bulky-weight is approximately the same as three strands of light-weight or one strand *each* of light- and medium-weight.

We Used:

BODY

MC—3 skeins of Zucca from Prism Yarns (9 oz; 340 yds), color Arroyo (5)

CC—Approx 1000 yds of assorted blending textures (3) (4) (5) (6)

TRIM

2 skeins of Rococo from Prism Yarns (3 oz; 72 yds), color Garden (4)

2 skeins of ¼" Sparkle Ribbon from Prism Yarns (2½ oz; 95 yds), color Firefox (4)

2 skeins of Charmeuse from Prism Yarns (1¾ oz; 68 yds), color Orchard (4)

NOTE: We used approx ½ skein each of Rococo and ¼" Sparkle Ribbon in the body of the afghan, reserving 1½ skeins of each for the trim. All the Charmeuse was used for the trim.

Gauge

6 sts and 16 rows = 4" in patt

Corded Rib Stitch

(Any number of sts)

Rows 1 and 2: Knit.

Rows 3 and 4: Purl.

Rep rows 1–4.

Preparation

Sort all the contrasting color yarns into three piles—A, B, and C—according to yarn size. Within each group, line up the colors loosely from lighter to darker. You will be working with one strand of main color and one, two, or three strands of contrasting color at all times. The main color will remain constant. The contrasting color yarns should change every one to six rows, with two to four rows being the most commonly repeated segments. Keep it random! A set, repeated pattern is not necessary. If you are using either B and C or all C yarns, try changing just one of the yarns in the mixture, continue for a few rows, and then change another. Use the colors that are loosely based on the light to dark arrangement, in slow moving waves; or use all the light, gradually introducing the medium and then darker colors for a dramatic throw that is shaded from corner to corner. It can be helpful to put each yarn in a zippered plastic bag, labeled with its size and its light, medium, or dark color placement.

Throw

- CO 3 sts. K1f&b at each edge EOR while working corded rib st.

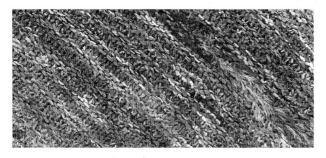

TIPS

- Here is an easy way to tell what the next row should be: Look at how many consecutive purl rows there are next to the needle. If there is one purl row facing as you begin the row, purl (to make a second row of bumps); if there is one purl row on the back side, knit. If there are two purl rows facing as you begin the row, knit. If there are two purl rows on the back side, purl.

- An easy way to keep track of your increases is to always shape on the first row of the knit or purl; that is, on row one or three. Or, you can place a safety pin on the right side at the beginning. Increase when the pin is there; work an even row when the pin is at the other end.

- Work to approx 54" measured along 1 edge, ending with WS row.

- **Shape length:** K1f&b at beg and K2tog at end of EOR. Work to approx 70", shape as follows: ssk at beg, work to last 2 sts, K2tog. Rep until 3 sts rem, BO.

Finishing

- With ¼" Sparkle Ribbon and crochet hook, work 2 rnds sc around entire edge, working 3 sts in each corner and laying piece flat periodically to make sure edges are even.

- Cut ¼" Sparkle Ribbon and attach Charmeuse, and work popcorn row around entire edge as follows: Ch 3 and make 2 dc in same space as ch 3, remove loop from hook, reinsert hook in top of ch 3 and pull dropped loop through this st (popcorn made). *Ch 2, sk next sc, work 3 dc in next sc, drop loop and reinsert in top of first dc, pull loop through this st (popcorn made). Rep from * across edge to corner, make 3 popcorns in a row without skipping sts while continuing to ch 2 between popcorns (corner turned), and rep for each edge and corner. Cut Charmeuse and attach Rococo, then work finished edge as follows: *Ch 4, work 1 sc between popcorns and into the ¼" Sparkle Ribbon st below, rep from * around. Fasten off.

- **Tassels:** Using rem ¼" Sparkle Ribbon, cut 8 pieces, 16" long. With rem ribbons and any other leftover yarns that do not ravel, wrap 120 to 160 strands around an 8" book. Tie 1 of Sparkle Ribbons tightly around center of each bundle of tassel yarn, then fold at tie and wrap another

Sparkle Ribbon tightly around bulk of tassel, about 1½" from top. Tie tightly and bury ends. With very sharp scissors, trim bottom of tassel, making a softly sculpted bottom by cutting middle longer and sides a bit shorter. Tie 1 tassel tightly to each corner, and bury ends of tie back into body of tassel.

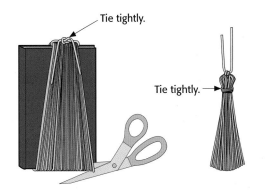

Tie tightly.

Tie tightly.

STRIPED CHEVRON AFGHAN

I have a typical stash full of yarn that I've fallen in love with. Most of those bags of yarn are not enough for a complete project. Interestingly, and you may very well find the same thing that I did, many of the colors are compatible. A number of the projects in this book explore different ways to use yarns together, allowing you to come up with a grand total of enough yarn for the project. Here is an afghan that can be big or small, depending on how many different yarns you want to use.

A 48" x 60" afghan on size 15 needles will require about 1,200 yards. If the yarns are thick (sizes 5 and/ or 6), you simply need a total of that many yards. If some of the yarns are thinner, you can double them or combine them with other strands to get to the correct gauge. In that case, you will need the same yardage of each yarn you plan to combine. If you have a combination of thick and thin yarns, treat them as groups: If you have four textures, you will require approximately 300 yards per texture for evenly spaced stripes. If some of those textures are multiple strands, you will need the same yardage for each individual yarn. You can use different amounts of yarn by changing the frequency of each stripe.

Before designing the stripes for this afghan, I tried a simple stockinette stitch swatch on size 15 needles, knitting each yarn for six rows. This allowed me to see if the yarns were compatible with each other—the swatch may feel flimsy or thick in certain sections. This doesn't mean you cannot use those yarns together; it simply means you may want to use fewer rows of each yarn or to space them differently. I found that Genie was the thickest yarn and much denser than the others. That suggested using it in much smaller stripes of one or two rows only. Zucca, of which there was plenty in one color, was the most compatible with Genie in gauge but much softer in hand, which allowed more rows. The other yarns were sometimes flimsy, sometimes slinky, and since I had limited yardage, they were better used as accents.

The next swatch was in a garter slip-stitch pattern on size 15 needles, which meant using only one row of each yarn and cutting and tying at each row to form fringe. The slip-stitch pattern didn't really show up amidst all of the texture, so I decided that simplicity would be better, something with more distinct stripes to separate the textures. That led me to the subtle chevron stripe.

These are the yarns that I had and their yardages:

Yarn	Total Yards
Zucca Olive	639
Zucca Sea	142
Genie	297
Essence	720
Huaca	750
Segue	240

I started with more Genie, but I used almost an entire ball in swatching. The final swatch used a simple garter and stockinette combination on size 15 needles with a slight bit of feather-and-fan shaping to make the stripes more interesting. I decided to run the stripes vertically and to cut and tie the yarns at the end of each row to make fringe as the piece was worked. There was quite a bit more yardage available than was needed for the throw, so I was able to switch the stripes around for the most pleasing effect. Alternating soft Zucca with stiffer Genie provided a more even hand throughout the throw. Tossing

in small amounts of the other textures gave a rich, opulent look, and every one of the yarns made an interesting fringe.

The stripe sequence has a bit of a random feel to it, with fewer stripes of the yarns I had less of. I wanted Genie to have as much presence as possible, so I repeated it in one of the garter sections as well as in every stockinette section. Not to worry about the yarn left over—like starter for yummy sourdough bread, I can use the leftovers to design another project! *Hmmm, pillows might be nice . . . .*

Size

Approx 48" x 60", excluding fringe

Materials

Approx 1200 yds *total* of medium-, bulky-, and super-bulky-weight yarns (4) (5) (6)

Size 15 needles or size required to obtain gauge

We Used:

Zucca from Trendsetter Yarns (50 g; 72 yds) in the following amounts and colors:

6 skeins of 707 Olive (5)

2 skeins of 518 Sea (5)

8 skeins of Genie from Trendsetter Yarns (50 g; 33 yds); color 4071* (6)

3 skeins of Essence from Trendsetter Yarns (50 g; 72 yds), color 501 (5)

3 skeins of Huaca from Prism Yarns (2 oz; 75 yds), color Tumbleweed† (4)

2 skeins of Segue from Trendsetter Yarns (100 g; 120 yds), color 118‡ (6)

I used almost every yard available, which meant piecing in the middle of rows. If you don't want to piece, get an extra skein.

†*Huaca is discontinued, but any medium-weight bouclé could be substituted.*

‡*I used only a few yards of the 2nd ball.*

NOTE: The yardage for all of the above comes out to somewhat more than the 1200 yards—about 1400, but since few balls were used in their entirety, the amount left over accounts for the extra yards.

Gauge

2 reps (22 sts) = 10" and 24 rows = 7" in chevron patt and stripe sequence

Chevron Pattern (Multiple of 11)

Rows 1–5: Knit.

Rows 6, 8, and 10 (RS): *K2tog, K2, K1f&b in each of next 2 sts, K3, ssk, rep from * to end.

Rows 7, 9, and 11: Purl.

Row 12: Rep row 6.

Rep rows 1–12.

Afghan

NOTE: At end of each row, cut a tail approx 8" long and tie next yarn to this with an overhand knot, snugging knot up close to needle and forming fringe as you work. When working two rows of same yarn, cut and tie between rows for fringe.

- With Essence, CO 132 sts and work chevron patt in stripe sequence:

  CO and row 1: Essence

  Rows 2 and 3: Segue

  Rows 4 and 5: Huaca

  Rows 6 and 7: Zucca Olive

  Rows 8 and 9: Genie

  Rows 10 and 11: Zucca Olive

  Rows 12 and 13: Huaca

  Rows 14 and 15: Zucca Sea

  Rows 16 and 17: Essence

  Rows 18 and 19: Zucca Olive

  Rows 20 and 21: Genie

  Rows 22 and 23: Zucca Olive

  Rows 24 and 25: Genie

  Rows 26 and 27: Segue

  Rows 28 and 29: Huaca

  Rows 30 and 31: Zucca Olive

  Rows 32 and 33: Genie

  Rows 34 and 35: Zucca Olive

  Rows 36 and 37: Huaca

  Rows 38 and 39: Essence

  Rows 40 and 41: Huaca

  Rows 42 and 43: Zucca Olive

  Rows 44 and 45: Genie

  Rows 46 and 47: Zucca Olive

  Rep from beg, working 2 rows of Essence instead of CO plus 1 row.

- Work to approx 48", finishing with row 5 of chevron patt. BO all sts. Trim fringe evenly.

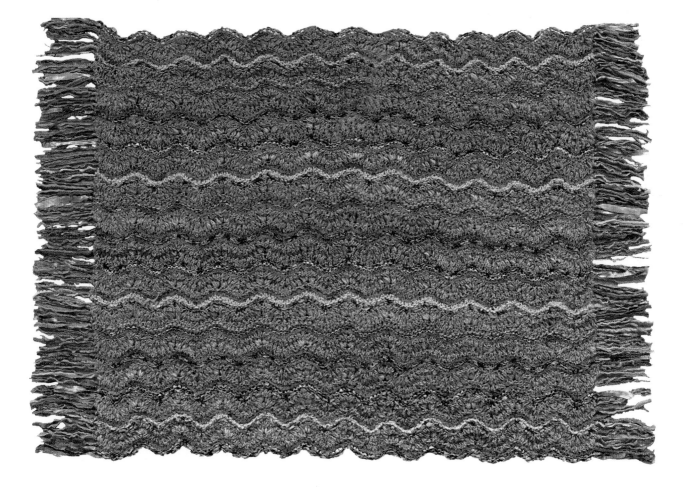

RECYCLED SARI SILK PILLOWS

This interesting yarn is recycled sari silk from Nepal. When I first saw it years ago at a knitting market, I fell in love with the look and the concept (we knitters are inveterate recyclers—nothing ever goes to waste!). I purchased a variety of colors, both solid and tweedy. No two tweed skeins were the same, and I got several closely related and compatible solids. As I wound the yarn into a ball I noticed little curls where the yarn twisted back on itself—a telltale sign that the knitting might become pulled out of square. I worked a stockinette-stitch swatch and found that, indeed, the yarn was tightly spun and the swatch veered off to the right. Switching to garter stitch corrected the problem. The yarn was also fairly coarse, not what one would expect from silk. I know that the current sari silks are much softer and less likely to pull out of square, so the spinners have improved their technique.

But, I still had this silk and didn't want it to go to waste, so I decided a group of pillows would be just right. I was fortunate to have in my fabric stash a woven silk from India that I thought would look perfect as pillow backs. When I looked more closely at the fabric I found that in fact it was woven from recycled sari silk! A perfect match, indeed.

Bias Garter Pillows

As the name suggests, these pillows are purposely knit on the bias. Knitting on the bias is achieved by beginning in one corner, with one stitch, increasing to the desired size, and then decreasing back down to one stitch. There are lots of variations, but I chose to keep these simple, in garter stitch, to avoid any further distortion from the yarn that is spun too tightly.

Why knit on the bias? The stripes take on a dynamic, diagonal direction, much more interesting than static horizontal or vertical orientation. One of the beautiful aspects of bias knitting is that gauge isn't critical, because you're working to a measurement. We do give a suggested gauge, because a pillow should be knit tightly enough to keep the filling from showing. It would be easy to substitute other yarns, because anything that is fairly firm will work well.

Each 18" pillow top took approximately 250 yards plus another 100 yards for edgings. You can pick as many or as few colors as you like, but I think the more the merrier!

From top to bottom:
Blended striped pillow,
Boldly striped pillow,
Mitered pillow

CANCELING THE TWIST

Twisted and plied yarns are sometimes oversprung or twisted too tightly. When yarns are knitted, the relaxed strands seek to release the excess twist.

In stockinette stitch the release is all in the same direction, because the stitches are aligned in the same direction. As the energy is released, the knitting is pulled off square. The top and bottom will be in a straight line, but the sides will slant. Any stitch that uses knits and purls on the same surface, such as seed stitch, basket weave, or any textured stitch that has balanced numbers of knits and purls, will successfully cancel the off-center pull. So does garter stitch, which is essentially a row of knit alternated with a row of purl. Even though all rows are knitted, the work is being turned, and the face of the fabric is alternated knit and purl rows. Imagine garter stitch worked in the round—you would have to alternate a knit round with a purl round. Linen stitch, featured on page 24, is another good pattern stitch to use with tightly twisted yarn because the yarn floats that are worked on the right side of the fabric will cancel the pull.

Pillow Top

Size

Approx 18" x 18", excluding edging

Materials

Approx 250 yds of medium-weight yarn* for 1 pillow top, in assorted colors (4)

Approx 100 yds of medium-weight yarn for edging, in assorted colors (4)

Size 7 needles or size required to obtain gauge

Size G crochet hook

18" pillow form or finished pillow

18" zipper (optional)

*I used skeins of recycled silk that I purchased years ago when it was first introduced. See Himalaya Yarn and Mango Moon in "Resources" on page 127 for information on purchasing recycled silk yarn.

Gauge

18 sts and 36 rows = 4" in garter st

Blended Striped Pillow

My favorite technique of one-row stripes is used here to create a fabric of all-over blended colors.

NOTE: Select three different colors: A, B, and C. I used one tweed multicolor and two solids. Cast on with A, and work foundation row. Begin alternating one row of each yarn as described on page 20 and continue for the entire pillow top. You may also use more than three colors. Simply drop A and add D, then later on drop B and add E, and so on.

Pillow

- Place a slipknot on the needle.

  Foundation row: Knit into front of slipknot, knit into back of slipknot, and knit into front of slipknot again—3 sts.

  All WS rows: Knit.

  All RS rows: K1f&b, knit to last 2 sts, K1f&b, K1.

> **TIP:** Place a safety pin near the edge on the surface of the right side. When the pin is at the beginning of the row, it is the right side. When the pin is at the end, it is the wrong side.

- Work to 17" along 1 edge (not sts on needle, but selvage edge).
- Beg dec:

  All WS rows: Knit.

  All RS rows: K1, ssk, work to last 3 sts, K2tog, K1.

  Cont to work WS and RS rows until 1 st rem. Fasten off.

Edging

- With crochet hook and any color, work 1 rnd sc around pillow, working 3 sts in each corner. With another color, work 2nd rnd sc.
- With 2 more colors, work hdc rnd as follows: Fasten on 1 color. Wrap once, insert into same st, wrap and pull through edge but not through loops. Drop this color and add another, wrap and draw through 2 loops. *Wrap once and insert into next st, wrap and pull through edge, change colors, wrap and pull through both loops*, rep from * to * around, working 3 sts in each corner.
- Work 1 rnd sc with any color, working 3 sts in each corner.
- Work 1 rnd rsc with any color, working 1 st in each st.

Boldly Striped Pillow

Select as many colors as you wish. We used five solids and one tweed multicolor. To avoid burying the ends later, weave them into the back as you knit. These stripes use Fibonacci numbers to create a more graphic statement.

Pillow

- Work as for Blended Striped Pillow in Fibonacci stripe sequence as follows:

  8 rows Brown

  5 rows Olive

3 rows Violet

2 rows Tweed

1 row Rust

2 rows Gold

3 rows Rust

5 rows Tweed

8 rows Violet

13 rows Olive

8 rows Brown

- Rep stripe sequence as needed to get to 17" along 1 side, then beg dec as for Blended Striped Pillow on page 76. Fasten off.

Edging

- **Rnds 1–5:** With crochet hook, work 5 rnds sc around pillow edge, working 3 sts in each corner. Make each rnd a different color or use same color.

- **Rnd 6:** Attach contrasting color and work *1 sc in next st, 1 sc in next st in 2nd rnd down, 1 sc in next st, 1 sc in next st in 4th rnd down, rep from *, watching spacing as you near corner so that each corner has 2 sc in st before corner, 1 sc in 4th rnd in corner st, then 2 sc in next st (you can skip a st or two as you approach corner to make spacing work out).

- **Rnd 7:** Work 1 rnd rsc with any color.

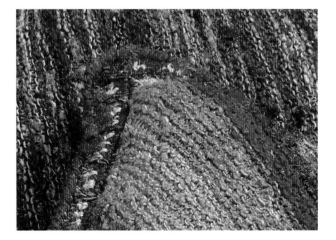

Mitered Pillow

I used the leftovers from the Blended Striped Pillow and the Boldly Striped Pillow for this mitered pillow. Working a central decrease bends the stripes for a nice complement to the other pillows.

Pillow

- CO 126 sts. K63, pm, K63.

- Working in garter st, alternate different colors as desired:

  Row 1: Knit to last 2 sts before marker, ssk, sm, K2tog, work to end.

  Row 2: Knit.

  Rep rows 1 and 2 until 2 sts rem, K2tog and fasten off.

Edging

- **Rnd 1:** With crochet hook and any color, work 1 rnd sc, working 3 sts in each corner.

- **Rnd 2:** Ch 3, work 1 hdc in next st, tie on contrasting color and with CC, *in next st (wrap and pull through edge) twice, wrap and pull through all loops on hook (small bobble made), with first color work 1 hdc in each of next 2 sts, rep from *, working (hdc, bobble, hdc) in each corner (you can work an extra st or skip a st to get the sequence correct for corner).

- **Rnd 3:** Work 1 rnd sc with any color, working 3 sts in each corner.

- **Rnd 4:** Work 1 rnd rsc with any color, working 1 st in each st.

- **Rnd 5:** With any color, attach at corner, *ch 4, sc in top of bobble from rnd 2, rep from * around.

PILLOW ASSEMBLY

There are several ways to finish pillows once the knitting and edgings are completed.

- You can make two identical (or different) pillow tops and work the edging on only one of them. Sew three sides together inside the edging, and insert a pillow form. Sew the last side closed. I like to use a pillow form that is one size larger than the finished measurement of the knitted top, because the knitting will stretch a bit and the form will fill the corners well, giving a nice plump look to the pillow. The flanged edges will hide any seams nicely, because you can stitch in the "ditch" formed by the crochet rows.

- If you like, you can insert a zipper on one side so that you can easily remove the pillow form to facilitate cleaning. I find that my knitted pillows actually get used, and being able to easily hand wash them is a plus. The zipper will be hidden under the flange.

- A fabric back is also a nice choice but requires some sewing skills. I like to machine stitch mine, again because I actually use the pillows and they hold up better. The ditch formed by the crochet rows provides a perfect place for machine stitching that doesn't show. The fabric can be turned under at the edges, and the pillow top can be top-stitched to the fabric. Or you can insert the zipper first, and then open the zipper and twist the edges around to form an actual seam. Don't sew all the way into the corners; leave long tails of thread so that you can hand stitch the corners shut.

- Another option is to buy an attractive finished pillow and simply sew your knitted top on! Again, if you have worked the flanged edges, you can sew by hand to the pillow through one of the ditches, and no one will ever see the stitching.

SCRAP-YARN TEDDY BEAR

Well, what could be more fun than this very touchable teddy? I have adapted the pattern from one that came to me years ago from an unknown source—it had been written and rewritten as it was passed along. I am very conscious of copyright issues, so although I adapted some of the details and shaping, the pattern is completely resized and also tweaked here and there. Thank you to the unknown designer who wrote the original—I owe you one!

What I have always liked about this particular teddy is the shaping that makes a bear that actually sits, with legs that are in front of him. Although there are lots of little pieces that need to be assembled, I think it's worth the effort for the truly cylindrical limbs with their contrasting paws and feet. Once I mastered the mattress-stitch seaming method years ago, I have never minded sewing seams. There are lots of great teddy patterns available, so if you really dislike seams, pick another and use the same stash concepts I've recommended.

Sizes

Small: approx 12" high
Large: approx 16" high

We Used:

Assorted medium-weight angora yarns for the small bear and a bulky nylon for the large bear. (4) (5)

Materials

MC—For body, head, legs, arms, and ear backs, approx 300 yds *total* of assorted colors in the following yarn weights: light, medium, bulky, or super-bulky (3) (4) (5) (6)

CC—For inner ears, muzzle, paws, and feet, approx 40 yds of contrasting color yarn in the same weight as MC

Size 4, 6, 8 or 10 needles, depending on yarn size

2 animal eyes

1 bag of stuffing

1 yard of stiff 4"-wide interfacing (the kind used in the head of draperies to hold pleats)

Gauge

The different sizes of bears are achieved through the gauge, not number of stitches, except for the arm and leg lengths, which are specified for each yarn type. Work with smaller-than-usual needles to make the

body dense enough that the stuffing doesn't show through.

Light-weight yarns and size 4 needles:

22 sts = 4" **(3)**

Medium-weight yarns and size 6 needles:

20 sts = 4" **(4)**

Bulky-weight yarns and size 8 needles:

17 sts = 4" **(5)**

Super-bulky-weight yarns and size 10 needles:

15 sts = 4" **(6)**

NOTE: If you wish to make a scrap-yarn bear like the one in the photo on page 81, you may prewind the yarn for ease of knitting. Wind approximately one to two yards of each yarn, cutting and tying on the next yarn, leaving a small tail. Make random lengths and use the colors randomly as well. Try to keep the color choices from the same part of the color-weight scale (see "In the Beginning: Sorting Your Stash" on page 5).

Leave long tails on all pieces to use for seaming.

Inc 1 st = K1f&b at beg and end of row.

Dec 1 st = ssk at beg of row and K2tog at end of row.

Body (Make 2 in MC)

- CO 10 sts. Purl 1 row.

- In St st, inc 1 st at beg and end of every row 10 times, then EOR 4 times. Work 3 rows even, then inc 1 st at beg and end of next row—40 sts.

- Work 14 rows even.

- Dec 1 st at beg and end of next row—38 sts. Work 3 rows even. Dec 1 st at beg and end of EOR 5 times, then every row 3 times. BO rem 22 sts.

Head (Make 2 in MC)

Cast on edge is top of head.

- CO 16 sts. Purl 1 row.

- In St st, inc 1 st at beg and end of every row 6 times, then EOR 3 times—34 sts.

- Work 15 rows even.

- Dec 1 st at beg and end of EOR 3 times, then every row 4 times. BO rem 20 sts.

Muzzle (Make 1 in CC)

- CO 8 sts. Purl 1 row.

- In St st, inc 1 st at beg and end of every row 3 times, then EOR 2 times—18 sts.

- Work 5 rows even.

- Dec 1 st at beg and end of EOR 2 times, then every row 3 times. BO rem 8 sts.

Inner Ears (Make 2 in CC)

- CO 12 sts. In St st, work 10 rows.

- Dec 1 st at beg and end of every row 4 times. BO rem 4 sts.

Ear Backs (Make 2 in MC)

- CO 19 sts. In St st, work 12 rows.

- Dec 1 st at beg and end of every row 3 times, then every row 2 times. BO rem 9 sts.

Legs (Make 2 in MC)

- CO 38 sts. In St st, work for 3 (4, 5, 6)".

- BO 3 sts at beg of next 2 rows, then BO 2 sts at beg of next 4 rows, then dec 1 st at beg and end of every row until 2 sts rem. BO 2 sts.

Feet (Make 2 in CC)

- CO 5 sts. Purl 1 row.

- In St st, inc 1 st at beg and end of every row 2 times, then EOR 2 times—13 sts.

- Work 3 rows even.

- Dec 1 st at beg and end of EOR 2 times, then every row 2 times. BO rem 5 sts.

Arms (Make 2 in MC)

- CO 20 sts. Purl 1 row.

  Row 1: K1, inc 1 st, K6, inc 1 st, K2, inc 1 st, K6, inc 1 st, K1—24 sts.

  Rows 2 and 4: Purl.

  Row 3: K1, inc 1 st, K8, inc 1 st, K2, inc 1 st, K8, inc 1 st, K1—28 sts.

  Row 5: K1, inc 1 st, K10, inc 1 st, K2, inc 1 st, K10, inc 1 st, K1—32 sts.

- Cont in St st until arm measures 3 (4, 5, 6)".

- BO 4 sts at beg of next 4 rows, then 3 sts at beg of next 4 rows. BO rem 4 sts.

Paws (Make 2 in CC)

- CO 3 sts.

- In St st, inc 1 st at beg and end of every row 3 times—9 sts.

- Work 3 rows even.

- Dec 1 st at beg and end of every row 3 times. BO rem 3 sts.

Finishing

- Sew sides and CO edge of body.

- Sew sides and CO edge of head. Run a thread around edge of muzzle and draw thread up to slightly shape muzzle. Stuff lightly and sew to head.

- Sew inner ears to ear backs, leaving bottom edge open and curling outside edges in a bit to fit. Stuff lightly and sew to head, placing edge of ear at end of shaping.

- Attach eyes to head.

- Stuff body and head. To stabilize neck, make a tight roll of interfacing. Make a depression in both head and body to accept roll. Insert roll and stuff around as needed.

- Sew head to body.

- Sew legs and arms into tubes.

- Sew paws to CO edge of arms. Stuff and sew arms to body, allowing the arms to be slightly tubular.

- Stuff and sew legs to body, sewing top of legs right along seam line of body so that legs can bend easily while bear sits. Voilà! C'est Teddy!

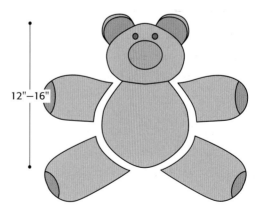

12"–16"

I love to knit. There, I said it. I also love to wear my knitted garments, and I take pleasure in seeing them worn by others. Lately the term "wearable art" has managed to work its way into the lexicon. I like to think that there is some art in everything we knitters make, so hearing that term always

Wearables

makes me smile a bit inside. My art training drives me to design clothing that looks good, so you will find careful attention to color use, stitch patterns, and yarn combinations in all my patterns. I also desire clothing that fits well, so you will find lots of shaping details in the following collection. More than that, I hope you are excited by many good ideas for using up that stash—so you can acquire more!

SLEEVELESS SHELL

Travel produces interesting opportunities to purchase unusual yarns. Since I am as much a yarn junkie as any of you, I have my fair share of beautiful skeins of odd yarns—never enough to do any one thing with! Amongst that stash were two incredible skeins of handspun angora and merino. One was light teal and the other sage green. Both had lots of natural-colored hairs, which made them slightly tweedy and muted. Each skein was eight ounces, but no yardage was given. I am sure the two skeins could have made a hat and scarf, but since I live in Florida, I was hoping for something more wearable.

The idea of a shaped, close-fitting sleeveless shell with a big, folded cowl neck appealed to me. The yarn is so soft, I would have no problem wearing it next to my skin, even in Florida. I loved this yarn worked in simple stockinette, but I didn't know the yardage and wasn't willing to risk getting partway through the garment only to find there was not enough. I decided to add a third element. Checkmate, a ribbon that goes from solid matte to shiny checkerboard, echoed the sage and teal while adding an accent of gold and purple. I tried it in half linen stitch with A, B, and C stripes, but eventually decided the simple one-row stripes in stockinette were, once again, a great solution.

I ran out of color A just as I finished the front. I decided to forgo the big, soft cowl in favor of a mock turtleneck and used B and C in one-row stripes to finish the neck. Since the stockinette neckline rolls a bit anyway, revealing the reverse side, it is not apparent that the row pattern is different from that in the body.

Sizes

Small (Medium, Large, X-Large)

Finished bust: approx 34 (38, 42, 46)" after seaming

Materials

Approx 450 (500, 550, 600) yds *total* of bulky- and/or super-bulky-weight yarns ⑤ ⑥

Size 10 needles

Size 11 needles or size required to obtain gauge

2 stitch holders

We Used:

Angora and Merino from Thistle Hill Farm (8 oz; 150 yds) in the following amounts and colors:

A—1 (1, 2, 2) skeins, color White Pine ⑤

B—1 (1, 2, 2) skeins, color Hydrangea ⑤

C—2 (3, 4, 4) skeins of Checkmate from Trendsetter Yarns (50 g; 70 yds), color 1045 ⑥

Gauge

12 sts and 18 rows = 4" in St st on larger needles, alternating 1 row of each yarn

Back

- With smaller needle and C, CO 54 (60, 66, 72) sts. Work 2 rows St st, then change to 1-row stripes (page 20) and larger needle and cont in St st, dec 1 st at each edge every 2" three times—48 (54, 60, 66) sts. Cont to 7", then inc 1 st at each edge every 1½" three times—54 (60, 66, 72) sts. Work to 11 (12, 13½, 14½)" from beg.

- **Shape armholes:** BO 4 sts beg next 2 rows. Dec 1 st at each edge EOR 6 times—34 (40, 46, 52) sts. Work even to 18 (19½, 21½, 23)" from beg. BO 9 (11, 13, 16) sts, place 16 (18, 20, 20) sts on holder, BO 9 (11, 13, 16) sts.

Front

- Work as for back to 17 (17½, 18½, 20)" from beg.

- **Shape neck:** Work across 14 (16, 18, 21) sts, place center 6 (8, 10, 10) sts on holder, and finish row. Working each shoulder separately, BO 2 sts at each neck edge twice, dec 1 st at each neck edge EOR once.

- Work until same length as back, BO all sts.

Finishing

- Sew shoulder seams.

- **Collar:** With smaller needles and C, K16 (18, 20, 22) sts from back holder, PU 15 sts to front neck, work 6 (8, 10, 10) sts from front holder, PU 15 sts to shoulder—52 (56, 60, 62) sts. In 3-yarn rotation (or 2-yarn rotation if you have run out of 1 yarn, as I did), work St st for 2", ending with row B. With C, work 4 rows St st, then with larger needle, BO all sts with C.

- **Armholes:** With smaller needle and C, PU 64 (68, 72, 76) sts along armhole edge. Work 2 rows St st, then BO all sts.

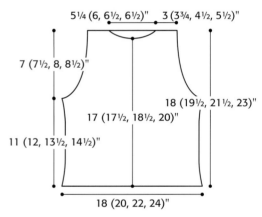

Knitted measurements before seaming

TRIO OF SWEATERS

Often we have plenty of yarns that look good together, but the gauges are not the same. This little sweater shows us that we can successfully use yarns of very different gauges together. The trick is to keep any one yarn from occurring for too many rows. In fact, the ideal is, once again, our little one-row stripes: A, B, C. Each yarn worked in a single row keeps the fabric from building up in areas that are too thick or too flimsy. The different weights balance rather magically. In our trio of sweaters, two yarns remain the same from sweater to sweater, while the third yarn changes. It's interesting that the change of one element can provide such a different look! When working this way, select a needle size that is about halfway between the suggested needles for the yarn types you're using. Diana usually knits on a 10½, while Sunshine, Biwa, and Dazzle work up on a size 6 needle.

Sleeveless Version

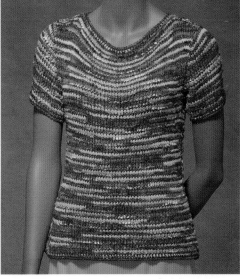

Short Sleeve Version 1

Sizes

Small (Medium, Large, X-Large)
Finished bust: approx 35 (38, 42, 46)"

Materials

Sleeveless Version

A—3 (4, 5, 5) skeins of Diana from Prism Yarns (2 oz; 55 yds), color Sagebrush (5)

B—2 (2, 3, 3) skeins of Dazzle from Prism Yarns (1 oz; 116 yds), color Arroyo (3)

C—2 (3, 3, 4) skeins of Biwa from Prism Yarns (1 oz; 68 yds), color Orchard (3)

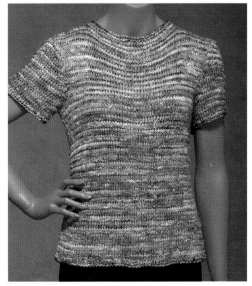

Short Sleeve Version 2

Cap Sleeve Version 1

A—4 (5, 5, 6) skeins of Diana from Prism Yarns, color Peacock ⑤

B—4 (5, 6, 6) skeins of Sunshine from Prism Yarns (1 oz; 65 yds), color Rio Fantasy ③

C—3 (3, 4, 5) skeins of Biwa from Prism Yarns, color Cantina ③

Cap Sleeve Version 2

A—4 (5, 5, 6) skeins of Diana from Prism Yarns, color Denim ⑤

B—3 (3, 4, 4) skeins of Slique from Prism Yarns (1½ oz; 93 yds), color Island ③

C—3 (3, 4, 5) skeins of Biwa from Prism Yarns, color Tumbleweed ③

All Versions

Size 8 needles or size required to obtain gauge

Size G crochet hook

Gauge

15 sts and 28 rows = 4" alternating 1 row of each yarn

Directions for Sleeveless Version

The sleeveless version has armholes that are cut in quite a bit. If you want more coverage, follow the pattern for the cap-sleeved version and omit the sleeves.

Back

- With A, CO 70 (76, 84, 92) sts. Working 1-row stripes (page 20), dec 1 st at each edge every 6th row 5 times—60 (66, 74, 82) sts. Work even for 6 (8, 10, 12) rows. Inc 1 st each edge every 8th row 3 times—66 (72, 80, 88) sts. Work until piece measures 13 (13½, 14, 15)" from beg.

- **Shape armholes:** BO 4 (5, 6, 7) sts at beg next 2 rows. Dec 1 st at each edge EOR 5 times. Dec 1 st at each edge every 4th row 4 (4, 5, 5) times—40 (44, 48, 54) sts. When body is 20 (21, 22, 23)", from beg, BO all sts firmly.

Front

- Work as for back to armhole, then shape armholes and neck.

- **Shape armholes and neck:** BO 4 (5, 6, 7) sts at beg of next 2 rows, dec 1 st at each edge EOR 2 times. Inc 1 st at each edge every 4th row 4 times (this forms neck drape)—62 (66, 72, 78) sts. When body is same length as back, BO all sts loosely.

Finishing

- Sew side seams.

- Working from outside edge toward neck, sew shoulder seam with invisible seaming from RS, pushing extra fabric of front to center and leaving a 6 (6, 6½, 7)" space along back neck.

- **Edging:** With crochet hook and B, work 1 rnd sc and 1 rnd rsc around neck edge. Rep for armholes and bottom edge.

Directions for Short Sleeve Versions 1 and 2

For those who like a bit more coverage, here's a version with a short sleeve. The armhole/neck shaping is a little different to accommodate the sleeve.

Back

- With A, CO 70 (76, 84, 92) sts. Working 1-row stripes (page 20), dec 1 st at each edge every 6th row 5 times—60 (66, 74, 82) sts. Work even for 6 (8, 10, 12) rows. Inc 1 st each edge every 8th row 3 times—66 (72, 80, 88) sts. Work until piece measures 13½ (14, 14½, 15½)" from beg.

- **Shape armholes:** BO 5 (5, 6, 7) sts at beg next 2 rows, dec 1 st at each edge EOR 6 times—44 (50, 56, 62) sts. When body measures 21 (22, 23, 24)" from beg, BO all sts firmly.

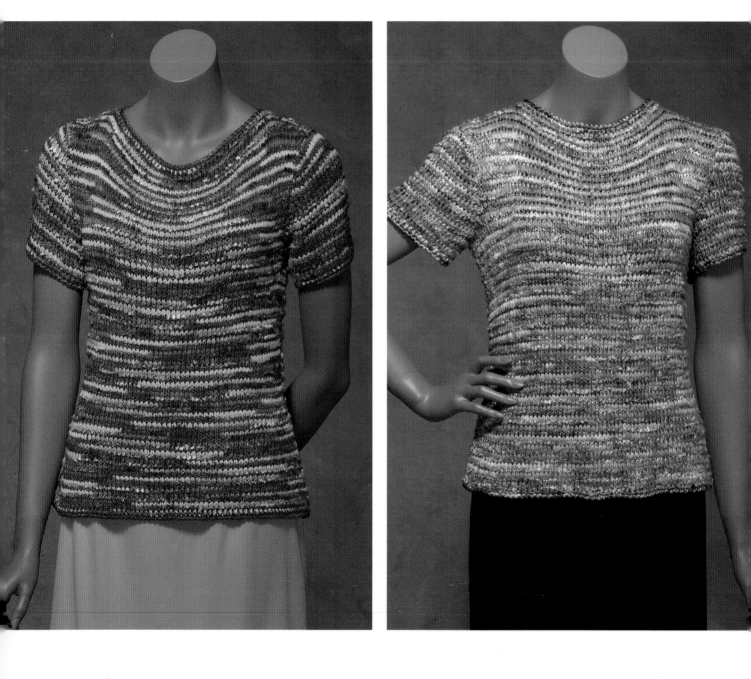

Front

- Work as for back to armhole, then shape armholes and neck.

- **Shape armholes and neck:** BO 5 (5, 6, 6) sts at beg next 2 rows. Dec 1 st at each edge EOR 2 times. Inc 1 st every 4th row 6 times—64 (70, 76, 84) sts. When body is same length as back, BO all sts loosely.

Sleeves

- With A, CO 52 (54, 56, 58) sts. Work 1-row stripes, and inc 1 st at each edge every 4th row 2 times. Work until sleeve measures 2 (2, 2½, 3)" long or desired length to underarm.

- **Shape cap:** BO 5 (5, 6, 6) sts at beg next 2 rows. Dec 1 st at each edge EOR to total length of 6 (6½, 7½, 8½)"—cap depth is 4 (4½, 5, 5½)". BO 5 sts at beg next 2 rows. BO all sts.

Finishing

- Sew side seams.

- Working from outside edge toward neck, sew shoulder seam with invisible seaming from RS, pushing extra fabric of front to center and leaving a 6 (6, 6½, 7)" space along back neck.

- Sew sleeve seam. Set sleeve into armhole edge.

- **Edging:** With crochet hook and B, work 1 rnd sc and 1 rnd rsc around neck edge and bottoms of sleeves and body.

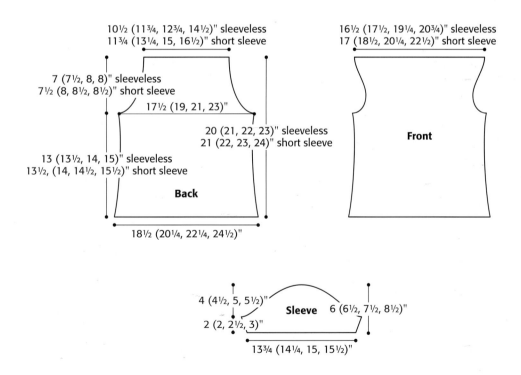

ALMOST-ENOUGH STRIPED TEE

It's fun to contemplate our stash over a period of time, until we find just the right use for a particular yarn. Frustration rears its ugly head when we have almost, but not quite, enough yarn to make the perfect garment. One solution is to find a compatible yarn and work stripes, which can be either subtle or strongly graphic. The following tees use the concepts discussed in the chapter "Strategies for Almost Enough" (page 23) to determine how often each stripe should appear. Swatch the yarns you contemplate using to be certain the knitted fabric has the look and feel that you like.

Ribbon Striped Tee

This tee grew out of a desire to use ¼" ribbon, which is fairly costly, in a more economical way. The ribbon feels crisp and is dyed in a painterly, muted way. The different choices of accent yarn illustrate that the stripes can either become so subtle they almost disappear or be very aggressive in texture and really stand out. I worked the second row of contrast in rib to make the texture of the yarn more important.

Sizes

Small (Medium, Large, X-Large)
Finished bust: approx 35 (38, 42, 46)"

Materials

Version 1

A—4 (5, 6, 7) skeins of ¼" Ribbon from Prism Yarns (2½ oz; 95 yds), color Periwinkles (4)

B—2 (2, 3, 3) skeins of Luna from Prism Yarns (1 oz; 58 yds), color Arroyo (4)

Version 2

A—4 (5, 6, 7) skeins of ¼" Ribbon from Prism Yarns (2½ oz; 95 yds), color Island (4)

B—1 (2, 2, 3) skeins of Super Dazzle from Prism Yarns (1 oz; 90 yds), color Thunderclap (3)

Both Versions

Size 8 circular needle and 10½ circular needle or size required to obtain gauge

Size G crochet hook

Version 1 with ¼" Ribbon and Luna

Version 2 with ¼" Ribbon and Super Dazzle

Gauge

14 sts and 20 rows = 4" in St st on larger needles

Ribbon Striped Pattern

(Multiple of 4 plus 2)

Rows 1, 3, 5, and 7: With A, knit.

Rows 2, 4, 6, and 8: With A, purl.

Row 9: With B, knit.

Row 10: With B, P2, K2 across to last 2 sts, P2.

Rep rows 1–10 for patt.

Back

- With smaller needle and A, CO 56 (60, 68, 76) sts and work 6 rows garter st. Change to larger needle and St st, inc 6 sts evenly spaced across next row—62 (66, 74, 82) sts. Purl 1 row.

- Beg ribbon striped patt with B (row 9). Cont in ribbon striped patt until piece measures 10½ (11, 12, 13)" from beg.

- **Shape armholes:** BO 5 (5, 7, 8) sts at beg next 2 rows. Cont in ribbon striped patt until piece measures 18 (19, 20½, 22)" from beg.

- **Shape shoulders and back neck:** BO 6 sts at beg next 2 rows (from armhole edge in), and AT SAME TIME, BO center 12 (12, 14, 14) sts. Working each shoulder separately, BO 6 sts at beg of each shoulder once. BO 3 sts at each neck edge once. BO 2 sts at each neck edge once. BO rem 3 (5, 6, 9) sts for each shoulder.

Front

- Work as for back to 14½ (15, 16, 17)" from beg.

- **Shape neck:** BO center 10 (10, 12, 12) sts, then working each shoulder separately, BO 3 sts at each neck edge once. BO 2 sts at each neck edge once. Dec 1 st at each neck edge once.

- When piece measures 18 (19, 20, 21)" from beg, shape shoulders as for back.

Sleeves

- With smaller needle and A, CO 36 (38, 40, 42) sts. Work as for body, and after garter band, inc 1 st at each edge EOR 6 (6, 7, 7) times—48 (50, 54, 56) sts.

- When sleeve measures 3½ (4, 4½, 5)" from beg, BO 2 sts at beg next 16 rows to shape cap. BO rem sts.

Finishing

- Sew shoulders with RS tog using crochet hook and slip st.

- Sew sleeves to armhole edge between the bound-off sts of armhole.

- Sew sleeve and side seam, tacking edge of sleeve to bound-off sts of armhole.

- **Edging:** With crochet hook and A, work 2 rnds sc around neck edge, then work 1 rnd rsc with B.

Fibonacci Striped Tee

A yarn stash often includes balls of different colors of the same yarn—the type of thing that goes on sale because they are the ends of dye lots. Dolcino, a wonderfully silky ribbon from Trendsetter Yarns, comes in a huge range of colors. I had lots of odd balls and picked a group of compatible colors. Fibonacci stripes provide a visual structure for using the colors successfully, as described on page 18 ("Design Tricks"). The end result is a more playful, sporty tee. Enjoy! (See facing page.)

Sizes

Small (Medium, Large, X-Large)
Finished bust: approx 35 (38, 42, 46)"

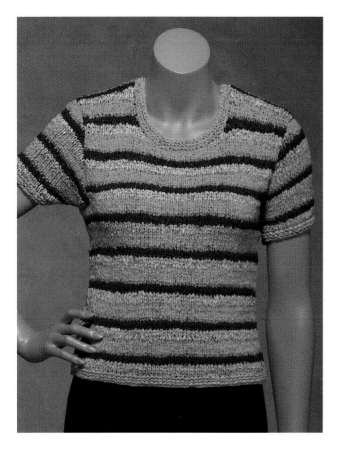

Materials

Dolcino from Trendsetter Yarns (50 g; 99 yds)
in the following amounts and colors*:

A—3 skeins, color Teal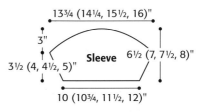

B—2 skeins, color Olive

C—2 skeins, color Violet

D—1 skein, color Magenta

E—1 skein, color Tan

Size 9 and 11 circular needles, or size
required to obtain gauge

Size G crochet hook

*As an alternative, try using 1 color. You will need
6 (6, 7, 8) skeins total of Dolcino.*

Gauge

14 sts and 20 rows = 4" in St st on larger
needles

Fibonacci Striped Pattern

5 rows with A

3 rows with B

2 rows with C

1 row with D

1 row with E

To make it easy on yourself when knitting, work back
and forth on circular needles so that you can slide the
work to the other end if you need to pick up a color
from that side.

Tee

- With size 9 needles and A, CO as for Ribbon
  Striped Tee. Work 6 rows garter st, then change
  to larger needles and B and following Fibonacci
  striped patt, work as for Ribbon Striped Tee in
  St st.

- **Edging:** With size 8 circular needle and A, PU
  26 (26, 28, 28) sts along back neck and 54 (56, 58,
  60) sts around front neck. Join and work 5 rnds
  garter st, beg with a purl rnd. BO all sts.

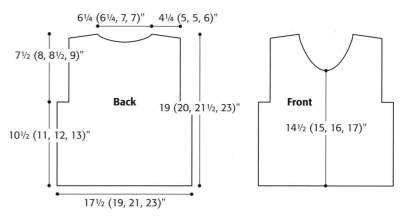

TWEEDY TEES

Here is another great way to use up lots of odds and ends. Once you have sorted your stash according to color and yarn weight, pick a group that looks promising. You might have to buy some additional skeins to fill out the yardage needs, but isn't that part of the fun?

The colors can be sorted within the group so that the tee is darker at the bottom and lighter at the top, or they can be used randomly. The seamless extension of the sleeves onto the body of this tee allows you to more accurately judge yarn quantities—no running out on the second sleeve. I have added a little texture with half linen stitch, which will be less striped and a bit tweedy in appearance.

> **TIP:** You can make this same tee with a medium-weight yarn by moving needle size and gauge size in from 20 stitches to 4" on size 7 needle to 18 stitches to 4" on size 9 needle and following the instructions for one size smaller than the desired finished size.

Sizes

Petite (Small, Medium, Large, X-Large)
Finished bust: approx 34 (38, 42, 46, 50)"

Materials

Body: Approx 800 (950, 1150, 1400, 1500) yds *total* of light-weight yarns ⓷

Trim: Approx 75 yds of ribbon or light-weight smooth yarn ⓷

Size 7 needles, or size required to obtain gauge

Size F crochet hook

We Used:

The following Prism yarns: ⓷

    2 skeins of Sunshine, color Cantina
    2 skeins of Biwa, color Splash
    1 skein of Tulle, color Jelly Bean
    1 skein of Flash, color Cantina
    1 skein of Slique, color Tropicana
    1 skein of Slique, color Jelly Bean
    1 skein of Dover, color Aruba
    1 skein of Collage, color Rio Fantasy

Everything Tee

The Everything Tee was worked with two rows of one yarn alternating with two rows of another for an inch or so. Then one yarn was dropped and replaced with another for an inch or so. Yarns were continuously changed as the tee was worked, but you can choose to work one-row stripes as described on page 20. This works especially well if you have many small bits of yarn, because the individual yarns become less important as the overall texture takes over. The pattern stitch does such a nice job of blending colors that two-row stripes still look great.

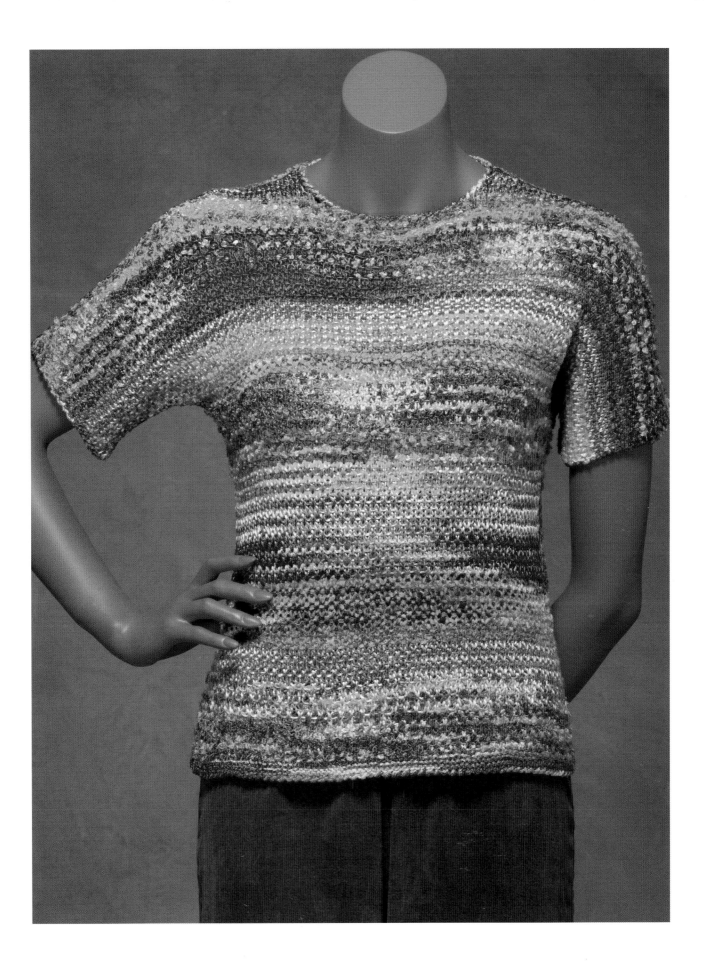

Gauge

20 sts and 28 rows = 4" in half linen st

Half Linen Stitch

(Even number of sts)

Row 1 (RS): *K1, slip 1 wyif, rep from * across.

Row 2: Purl.

Row 3: *Sl 1 wyif, K1, rep from * across.

Row 4: Purl.

Rep rows 1–4.

> **TIP:** If working with many different yarns, use two yarns at a time, working rows one and two with yarn A, then rows three and four with yarn B. Work for an inch or so, and then drop A, add C and work two rows B, and then work two rows C. Repeat, changing yarns as often as you wish. If shading your sweater from bottom to top, save half of each yarn for the other side. If using randomly, don't worry about where you change or about making the front and back match—your eye will never notice.

Back

- CO 86 (96, 106, 116, 126) sts and work 6 rows garter st.

- Change to half linen st and work until piece measures 11 (12, 13, 14, 15)" from beg.

- **Shape sleeves:** Inc 1 st at beg next 4 rows, then CO 2 sts at beg next 4 rows, then CO 8 sts at beg next 4 rows—130 (140, 150, 160, 170) sts.

- Cont in half linen st until piece measures 19 (20, 21, 22, 23)" from beg.

- **Shape shoulders and neck:** At shoulder edge, BO 10 sts at beg next 6 rows. BO 12 (10, 10, 10, 11) sts at beg next 4 rows. BO 0 (8, 12, 14, 18)

sts at beg next 2 rows, and AT SAME TIME after first 4 BO rows (or 2 steps on each side), shape neck: BO center 14 (14, 14, 16, 16) sts, then working each shoulder separately, BO 2 (2, 3, 3, 3) sts at each neck edge twice. Dec 1 st at each neck edge EOR 0 (1, 0, 2, 1) times.

Front

Work as for back, but beg neck shaping AT SAME TIME as shoulder shaping.

Finishing

- Sew shoulder and side seams, leaving a 3" slit at bottom of side seams.

- **Edging:** With crochet hook and trim yarn, work 1 rnd rsc around bottom, slit, sleeve, and neck edges.

Fur-Trimmed Tee

I had a bag each of two closely related colors. While a bag might have been enough to do a tee on its own, I thought a subtle tweed would be more fun and easier to coordinate with skirts or pants. A few yards of rabbit fur in a matching color became a great trim for the neck, which had shaping that was started earlier to make it more scooped.

Sizes

Petite (Small, Medium, Large, X-Large)
Finished bust: approx 34 (38, 42, 46, 50)"

Gauge

20 sts and 28 rows = 4" in half linen st

Materials

Size 7 needles or size required to obtain gauge

Size C and F crochet hooks

We Used:

Impuls from GGH (50 g; 125 yds) in the following amounts and colors:

A—3 skeins, color 11

B—3 skeins, color 12

6 yds rabbit fur, fake fur, or angora yarn

Tee

CO with A and work 6 rows garter st, then change to B and pattern st and work 2 rows. Alternating 2 rows of A and 2 rows of B, work as for Everything Tee, but for front, beg neck shaping at 16 (17, 18, 19, 20)" from beg.

Finishing

- Sew shoulder and side seams.

- **Edging:** With A and size F crochet hook, work 1 rnd sc. With size C crochet hook, work 1 rnd rsc around sleeve edges. With size C crochet hook, work 1 rnd sc around neck edge. Attach fur and with size F crochet hook, working 1 rnd slip st around neck edge.

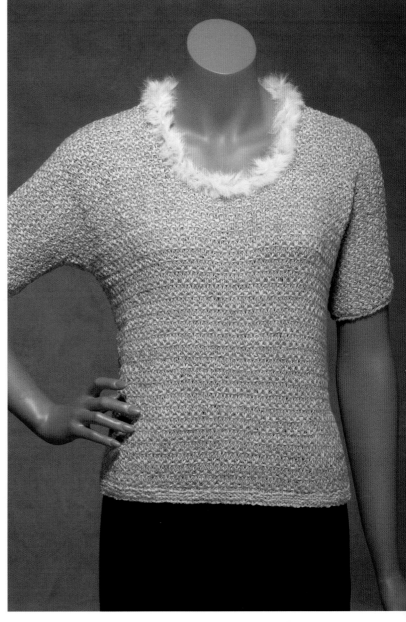

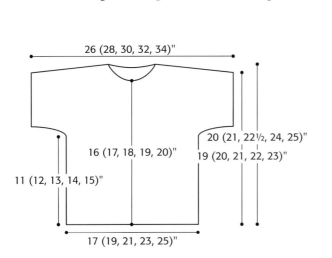

26 (28, 30, 32, 34)"

20 (21, 22½, 24, 25)"

16 (17, 18, 19, 20)"

19 (20, 21, 22, 23)"

11 (12, 13, 14, 15)"

17 (19, 21, 23, 25)"

PAINTER'S PALETTE PULLOVER

All knitters wind up with bits and pieces from other projects. Years of knitting can produce quite a substantial—and intriguing—pile of yarn. Because we tend to favor certain colors, many of those bits are compatible. Here's a sweater that uses a large variety of yarn-weight and color combinations, visually and functionally tied together with black wool. The yarns for the body range from light to super-bulky, and cover every imaginable type of strand, from simple plied wools through ribbons and various novelty yarns.

I separated the yarns first according to size and then according to color, and a plan became apparent. I used super-bulky or bulky yarns alone. I paired medium-weight yarns with light-weight yarns, and I also used light-weight yarns together in threes. No yarn or combination is used for more than a few rows, so even if the yarns are not exactly the same gauge, it doesn't matter.

The fabric is not densely knitted, which allows the simple rectangles of the body to have some drape. This lets us concern ourselves with the flow of color and texture instead of shaping. Crocheted edges stabilize the back and front, providing an important visual frame to the wild color and texture. Simple sleeves continue the framing, and the soft turtleneck forces shape into the plain rectangles. The sweater is designed to be oversized, allowing the soft bias fabric to drape around the body. Because the work is on the diagonal, you may choose to knit to whatever dimension you wish. Please note that the dimensions taken when laid flat will narrow quite a bit when worn, because of the bias construction.

Sizes

Small (Medium, Large, X-Large)
Finished bust: approx 46 (50, 54, 58)" (very oversized)

Materials

Body: Approx 22 (24, 28, 32) oz *total* of assorted yarns in the following yarn weights: fine, light, medium, and bulky. The total yardage needed if all strands are bulky-weight and used singly is approx 750 (800, 875, 950) yds. Strands used together require the same yardage for each strand. The larger the assortment of colors and texture, the richer the look. (2) (3) (4) (5)

Sleeves, trim, and collar: Approx 475 (500, 550, 600) yds of a smooth, bulky-weight yarn. We used 8 (8, 9, 10) skeins of Merino 12 from Lane Borgosesia (50 g; 66 yds), color 70 Black. (5)

Size 8 circular needle

Size 10½ circular needle or size required to obtain gauge

Size 11 circular needle or size required to obtain gauge

Size H crochet hook

NOTE: If you really wish to use up your stash, color block the solid areas with appropriate coordinating colors. Approximate yardages for each area are:

Trim: 90 (100, 120, 140) yards

Sleeves: 125 (150, 175, 200) yards each

Collar: 75 yards

Gauge

Body: 13 sts and 26 rows = 4" in garter st with assorted yarns on largest needle

Sleeves: 14 sts and 20 rows = 4" in St st with Merino 12 on midsized needle

NOTE: The body is worked on the diagonal, increased along both sides until the side edge is the desired length, and then worked even to the desired width, and then decreased to other corner. Garter stitch has no right side or wrong side, so place a safety pin at the beginning of the designated right-side rows. When the pin is at the beginning, you will know it is an increase row. When the pin is at the end, it is a work-even row. To anchor strands when changing yarn, work old and new strands together for two stitches, leaving a short tail on the wrong side.

Front/Back (Make 2)

- Sort your stash into yarn sizes first. Working according to color guidelines on page 7, sort each size into a color gradation. You might bag yarns within their groups, such as light-weight yarns in light, medium and heavy colors; or light-weight yarns in orange-to-red, purple-to-blue, and green-to-olive ranges. Then while knitting, it's a simple matter to reach for an appropriate yarn for next change.

- With largest needle and single strand of bulky-weight yarn, CO 1 st, knit in front, then in back, then in front of this stitch—3 sts.

Row 1 and all WS rows: Knit.

Row 2 and all RS rows: K1f&b, knit to last 2 sts, K1f&b, K1. For row 2, that means K1f&b, K1f&b, K1—5 sts. On subsequent rows there will be more sts in between the incs.

Rep rows 1 and 2, changing colors and yarns as desired, until 1 edge (measure holding upright to allow for downward stretch) is approx 20 (21, 23, 24)". Do not measure knitting from corner to needle; rather, measure along 1 edge.

- On RS rows, (inc at beg as established, work to last 3 sts, K2tog, K1) until width is approx 22 (24, 26, 28)" (measured lying flat) or desired width less 1".

- On RS rows, (K1, ssk at beg, work to last 3 sts, K2tog, K1) until 1 st rem. Fasten off.

- With RS facing you, crochet hook and black, work 2 rnds sc around each rectangle, working 3 sts in each corner, and spacing sts so that rectangle lies flat and sides are symmetrical.

- With RS of front and back tog, and with a smooth yarn, slip st shoulder seam tog through crochet sts, leaving a 9 (9, 9½, 10)"-wide opening for neck.

Sleeves

- With RS facing you, midsized needle and black, beg on front 7½ (8, 9, 10)" below shoulder seam, PU 26 (28, 32, 35) sts to shoulder seam, and 26 (28, 32, 35) sts to same point on back—52 (56, 64, 70) sts. Working in St st, on RS rows, dec 1 st at each edge (on 2nd and 3rd sts from edges) every 6th row 12 (13, 14, 15) times—28 (30, 36, 40) sts, ending on RS row. Sleeve should be approx 15 (16, 17, 18)".

- Change to smallest needle and dec 6 (6, 10, 12) sts evenly spaced across next row—22 (24, 26, 28) sts. Change to K1, P1 ribbing for 1", then BO very loosely in patt. Rep for other sleeve.

Collar

- With RS facing you, smallest circular needle and black, PU 28 (28, 30, 32) sts on front and 28 (28, 30, 32) sts on back—56 (56, 60, 64) sts. Join and work K1, P1 ribbing in the rnd for 2".

- Change to midsized circular needle and cont ribbing for 1".

- Change to largest circular needle and cont ribbing for 4"—7" total. BO all sts very loosely in patt (you may wish to use a size 13 needle).

Finishing

- Sew side and sleeve seams, leaving a slit at side hem of approx 6" if desired.

- With crochet hook and black, work 1 rnd rsc around bottom edge and side slits.

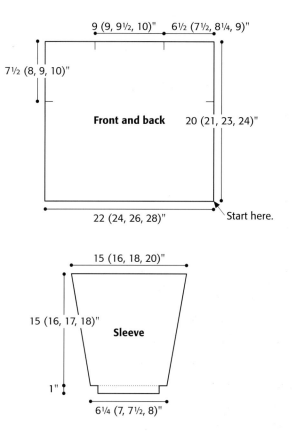

DOWN UNDER CARDIGAN OR PULLOVER

Many knitters enjoy working on a circular needle from the neck down, because there are almost no seams to sew and minimal finishing is required. Pullovers and cardigans can be worked with equal ease; a pullover is worked in the round, while a cardigan is worked back and forth on a circular needle, accommodating the large number of stitches and leaving the fronts open. A great thing about working from top to bottom is that the entire body grows at once, and you needn't be concerned about matching fronts to backs, or sleeves to armholes. When a yarn is used up, no problem; just continue with other yarns.

DESIGN NOTE

Often garments worked from the top down become too full in the sleeves, so I have made a subtle design change to control that fullness. For about the first half of the raglan shaping, body and sleeves are increased at the same rate. For the balance of the shaping, the sleeves are increased at half the rate of the body; that is, they are increased every fourth row (or round) instead of every *other* row (or round). The result is a slimmer, more fitted look. If you like a fuller sleeve, simply continue to increase at the same rate as the body.

Forest Glen Cardigan

This cardigan uses one strand of kid mohair held with an ever-changing array of novelty yarns and components. The added yarns were bits and pieces left over from various projects, along with several whole balls. The mohair unifies them in both color and weight, because they are not exactly alike in size. If you like, you can tie bits and pieces together before knitting, allowing the changes to happen randomly as in our teddy bear shown on page 81. Or, keep them handy in zipper-lock plastic bags, and grab one every few rows. Or, arrange them in a color story, working one-row stripes as on page 20 while always including the mohair. You can then change from A, B, C to B, C, D, and then to C, D, E and so on, and achieve a gradated, blended look.

Sizes

Small (Medium, Large, X-Large, XX-Large)
Finished bust: approx 38 (42, 45, 48, 52)"

Materials

MC—7 (8, 9, 9, 10) of Kid Mohair from Prism Yarns (1 oz; 125 yds), color Khaki ⬚

CC—Approx 850 (950, 1075, 1125, 1200) yds *total* of assorted light-weight yarns in assorted colors ⬚

Size 9 circular needle (40")

Size 11 circular needle or size required to obtain gauge

2 large stitch holders

8 stitch markers

Gauge

14 sts and 20 rows = 4" in St st on larger needles with 1 strand each MC and CC held tog

NOTE: You may wish to make your project one size larger to allow for the clothing that will be worn underneath a cardigan.

Body

- With larger needle and 1 strand each of MC and CC held tog, CO 36 (40, 44, 46, 50) sts. Purl back and pm as follows: P1, pm, P2, pm, P4 (5, 6, 6, 7), pm, P2, pm, P18 (20, 22, 24, 26), pm, P2, pm, P4 (5, 6, 6, 7), pm, P2, pm, P1.

- Turn and inc by K1f&b in st before and after every pair of markers—8 incs made. Always keep 2 sts between each pair of markers—visually, there will be 3 sts lined up at each inc point. Cont to make these same incs EOR and AT SAME TIME inc the neck sts once every 4th row 8 (9, 10, 11, 12) times.

- Work back and forth on circular needle to 5 (5½, 6, 6½, 7)" measured diagonally along the raglan inc, then work incs on front and back as established on EOR but work incs on sleeves every

4th row. Work until there are 62 (68, 72, 76, 82) sts between markers on back. The piece should be approx 9 (9½, 10, 10½, 11)", measured diagonally along raglan inc. If your work is within ½" of measurement for your size, cont. If your armhole has gotten too deep, rip back as needed, and add extra sts to number CO at underarm as directed below. If armhole is not deep enough, work a few more inc rows and take extra sts away from underarm CO.

- Move sleeve sts from between markers onto holder as follows: Work across 1 front, remove marker, K1, sl next st to first holder, remove marker, sl sleeve sts to first holder, remove marker, sl 1 st to first holder; using cable CO, CO 6 (6, 7, 7, 9) sts for underarm, K1, remove marker, work across back, remove marker, K1, sl next st to second holder, remove marker, sl sleeve sts to second holder, remove marker, sl 1 st to second holder, using cable CO, CO 6 (6, 7, 7, 9) sts for underarm, K1, remove marker, work across second front—134 (148, 158, 168, 182) sts.

- Work back and forth to 17 (18, 18½, 19, 20)", then change to smaller needle and work K1, P1 ribbing for 1". BO all sts loosely in patt.

Sleeves

- Place sleeve sts onto needle, then cable CO 3 (3, 4, 4, 5) sts, work across sleeve sts. Cable CO 3 (3, 4, 4, 5) sts at beg next row.

- Working in St st as for body, dec 1 st each edge every 6th row 11 (12, 13, 14, 15) times. When 15 (15½, 16, 17, 17½)" from sleeve CO, dec 3 sts evenly spaced across row, then with smaller needle work 1" of K1, P1 ribbing. BO all sts in patt.

Finishing

- Sew any seams necessary.

- **Neck and front band:** With smaller needle and 1 strand each of MC and CC held tog, beg at lower-right front, PU 58 (60, 62, 66, 68) sts to beg of neck, 18 (20, 22, 24, 26) sts to beg of sleeves, 4 sts across sleeve top, 22 (24, 26, 28, 30) sts along back, 4 sts along sleeve, 18 (20, 22, 24, 26) sts to end of neck, 58 (60, 62, 66, 68) sts to bottom—182 (192, 202, 216, 226) sts. Work 3 rows K1, P1 ribbing (beg with a purl st since you are on WS). Mark left side for 6 buttons. On next row, work buttonholes on right front to correspond to marks on left side. When last buttonhole is worked, at beg of neck, inc 2 sts in a row (to maintain K1, P1 ribbing), then rep this inc at left front neck. Work 3 more rows ribbing, then BO all sts in patt. Maintain an even tension, not too tight or too loose. Check every few inches to make sure that band is lying flat—not pulling up or wavering.

NOTE: See instructions on page 124 to calculate perfect bands if your length is different from ours.

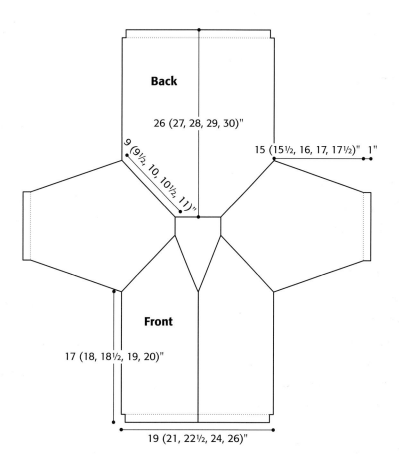

Back

26 (27, 28, 29, 30)"

9 (9½, 10, 10½, 11)"

15 (15½, 16, 17, 17½)"   1"

Front

17 (18, 18½, 19, 20)"

19 (21, 22½, 24, 26)"

Misty Meadow Pullover

Our long-sleeved pullover uses a strand of kid mohair with an array of four different multicolors of thin nub rayon. The colors were arranged from lightest to darkest and then used up as the sweater was knit from the top down. Once you have joined for circular knitting, you can make a good guess as to how much of each color to save for the sleeves. Use as many or as few colors as you like, finishing each one completely before going on to the next. It doesn't even matter where in the body you change to the new yarn— because the colors are softly graded, the jump will be subtle. To achieve a truly ombre look (with tones that shade into one another), alternate a row of the new color and the old for an inch or so, which will result in very subtle gradations from one color to another. Save one skein of the first color for the collar, which looks great standing up or rolled over.

Sizes

Small (Medium, Large, X-Large, XX-Large)
Finished bust: approx 38 (42, 45, 48, 52)"

Materials

MC—Approx 700 (750, 825, 900, 1000) yds *total** of assorted light-weight yarns 🔒

CC—Approx 700 (750, 825, 900, 1000) yds *total** of assorted light-weight yarns 🔒

Size 9 circular needle

Size 11 circular needle or size required to obtain gauge

2 stitch markers

Approx total yardage is for using 1-color MC and 1-color CC.

We Used:

MC—6 (6, 7, 8, 9) skeins of Kid Mohair from Prism Yarns (1 oz; 125 yds), color Periwinkle 🔒

CC—Biwa from Prism Yarns (1 oz; 68 yds) in the following amounts and colors:

2 (2, 3, 3, 4) skeins, color Fog 🔒

4 (4, 5, 5, 6) skeins, color Meadow 🔒

4 (4, 5, 5, 6) skeins, color Garden 🔒

3 (3, 4, 4, 5) skeins, color Tahoe 🔒

Gauge

14 sts and 20 rows = 4" in St st on larger needles with 1 strand each MC and CC held tog

Body

- Establish raglans as for cardigan, but instead of inc for V neck, inc 1 st at each neck edge every 4th row 2 times, then every other row 3 times.

- On row 16, CO 6 (8, 10, 12, 14) sts—the number of sts necessary to make the front equal to the back. Join and cont in the rnd, working incs as established on both sides of each pair of markers.

- Divide for sleeves as for cardigan. Work body in the rnd for 13 (13½, 14½, 16, 17)".

- With smaller needle, work K1, P1 ribbing for 1". BO all sts loosely in patt.

- Work sleeves as for cardigan.

Finishing

- Sew any seams necessary.

- **Collar:** With RS facing you and smaller needle, PU 58 (62, 64, 66, 68) sts around neck edge. Work K1, P1 ribbing for 1½", then change to larger needle and cont in ribbing for another 3½". BO loosely in patt.

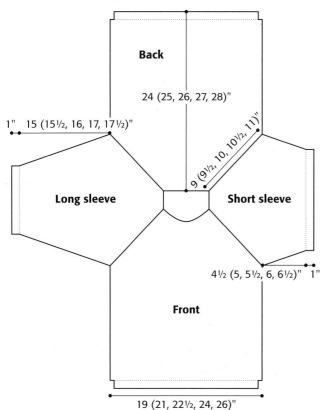

Carnival Tee

My sister, Karen, had a lot of odds and ends from other projects along with a few whole skeins, but no large quantity of any one yarn. I helped her sort according to color and yarn size, and then we picked a group that worked together. The gauge was correct for this top-down sweater, so with no further guidance from me, she followed the pattern and used the yarn any way she wished. As you can see in the photo above, the random stripes are great fun, and the variety of textures play off of each other very nicely. The yarns were mostly cotton, so she opted to make the sweater into a tee by shortening the sleeves. You can subtract about 150 yards from the yarn total needed if you choose to do the same.

TAILORED "EVERYTHING" JACKET

Here is a tailored jacket with a twist—exuberant, lively color and texture. I love to use menswear details such as welt pockets, shaped lapels, and a tweed stitch, and contrast them with the wild textures of novelty yarns. This is a great way to use up those odds and ends of bulky-weight yarns or to blend thin yarns to get them to the right gauge. Use the guidelines from the Blended Throw on page 66. To pump up the gauge, mohair would be a terrific blender. See "Mohair Is Our Friend" on page 25 for suggestions.

The jacket has such great lines that classic yarns would look equally good. If you have a variety of colors of smooth plied wools that are compatible in weight, this jacket would be perfect, because the linen stitch blends the colors beautifully. If the yarns are smaller than bulky-weight, hold multiple strands together to get the correct gauge. The strands could be different colors or the same. The possibilities are endless!

A close look shows the range of yarns used.

Sizes

Small (Medium, Large, X-Large)
Finished bust: approx 42 (46, 49, 52)" on the body

NOTE: The weight of the yarn causes the jacket to grow in length and to narrow in width. We have taken that into account when writing the pattern.

Materials

Body: Approx 1000 (1100, 1200, 1300) yds *total* of assorted bulky-weight yarns (5)

Trim: Approx 100 yds of smooth, medium-weight yarn (4)

Size 15 circular needle (40" or 47") or size required to obtain gauge

2 stitch holders

Size H crochet hook

Gauge

13 sts and 20 rows = 4" in linen st, alternating 3 yarns, 1 row each yarn

Make the pocket linings first to check your gauge.

COLOR REPEAT

Three yarns at a time are used for one row each, as described on page 20. Lay out the colors in a pleasing arrangement, alternating textures as well as colors. Work A, B, C for an inch or so, and then drop A and work B, C, D for another inch or so. Drop B and add E. Continue to move through the colors, using more of the yarns that have more yardage and less of the others. The more often the yarns change, the richer the texture and the less striped the fabric will be. To avoid building bulk at the front edges, make yarn changes somewhere in the middle of a row, burying the ends as you go. If you have a large amount of one yarn, use it throughout as A and change the other yarns.

Linen Stitch

(Even number of sts)

Row 1 (RS): *K1, slip 1 wyif , rep from * across.

Row 2: *P1, slip 1 wyib , rep from * across.

Rep rows 1 and 2.

Pocket Lining (Make 2)

With 1 of the yarns, CO 20 sts. Work linen st, alternating colors, for 8". Place sts on holder. Pockets should be just over 6" wide.

Body

Body is worked in 1 piece to armholes, then split for fronts and back and worked separately to shoulder.

- With smooth yarn, CO 160 (170, 182, 192) sts. Work linen st in 3-yarn rep as described above for 10".

- **Pocket opening:** Work 14 sts in patt, BO 20 sts, work to within 34 sts of end, BO 20 sts, finish 14 sts. On next row, work 14 sts, PU sts of pocket lining from holder, work across to other pocket opening, PU sts from 2nd holder, work across last 14 sts. Cont in patt and color rep to 19 (20, 21, 22)" (measured holding upright to allow for downward stretch), then shape lapel: K1f&b at each front edge every 6th row 10 times, AT SAME TIME after 16 rows (2 increases plus 4 more rows), divide for armholes: K1f&b, work across 42 (44, 47, 49) sts, K2tog, add another ball for back (or hold on needles and work back and 2nd front later), ssk, work across 70 (76, 82, 88) sts, K2tog, add another ball and ssk, work 42 (44, 47, 49) sts, K1f&b.

- Working each front and back separately, cont to inc at front edges as established, and dec 1 st each armhole edge on EOR. When armholes are 8½ (9, 9½, 9½)" deep, BO all front sts, and cont on back to 28½ (30, 31½, 32½)" from beg, then BO all sts, working 2 sts tog across as you go.

Right Sleeve

- With smooth yarn, CO 32 (34, 36, 38) sts. Work as for body (don't worry if sleeve does not match body exactly in color rep), and inc 1 st at each edge every 6th row 14 (14, 15, 15) times—60 (62, 66, 68) sts.

- Cont until sleeve measures 16½ (17, 18, 19)" or desired length to underarm seam.

- **Shape cap:** Dec 1 st at each edge on EOR to 8½ (9, 9½, 9½)", then cont to dec 1 st at end of WS rows, and dec 1 st at both ends of every RS row until 2 sts rem. BO rem sts. Rep for left sleeve, reversing shapings at top of cap.

Collar

- With smooth yarn, CO 76 (76, 78, 78) sts and work linen st in 3-yarn rep for 4", ending with row 2. Dec 1 st at each edge EOR 8 times. BO all sts.

Finishing

- Sew sleeves to fronts and back, with higher side of sleeve cap at back, and 2 bound-off sts at top left as part of neck.

- Sew side and sleeve seams.

- **Sewing collar to neck:** Sew with bound-off edge of collar placed along neck edge, between lapels, and short decreased edge placed along lapel (see diagram). Mark left side for 5 buttons.

- **Edging:** With WS facing you and with trim yarn and crochet hook, work 1 row sc up left front, around collar lapels and down left front, working chain-loop buttonholes at each marking. Work 1 row rsc in each st. Work 1 row sc and 1 row rsc along each pocket edge and around each sleeve bottom.

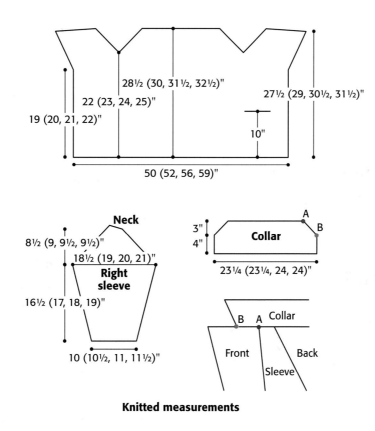

Knitted measurements

CONVERTIBLE CARDIGAN

Here's a fun idea for a cardigan. Make a shawl collar that attaches with a few small, hidden buttons on the fronts and you can change the collar at will! The collar doubles as a shaped scarf for wearing on its own. I've written the pattern for a large gauge, which is fun for stash because you can use up smaller amounts by adding strands to get up to the gauge.

I started with some wild handspun mohair for the collar and went searching through my stash for compatible colors. I found Cleo, a nub rayon novelty yarn with a bit of metallic. My initial swatch showed a fabric that was too thin to support the collar; also, I had only 10 balls (620 yards total), which would not be enough for a sweater body and sleeves. I next added a strand of Dune, a mohair blend with some metallic, in the same neutral colors. The gauge became much nicer, with a firmer hand. Because I only had 8 balls of Dune (720 yds), I was still a little leery of running out of yarn. I then added a strand of thin wool, Merino 8, and pumped the gauge up even more. I felt more confident that there would be enough yardage for the sweater I envisioned.

Just to be sure, I started with the sleeves, figuring the body length could be adjusted according to the amount of yarn left. As it turned out, every yard was used in the sweater, so I picked a different, coordinating yarn for the front edge trim. To tie it all together, I used the same trim yarn in a simple reverse single crochet at the sleeve and body hems.

Sizes

Small (Medium, Large, X-Large)
Finished bust: approx 38 (44, 48, 52)" on the body

NOTE: The weight of the yarn causes the cardigan to grow in length and to narrow in width. We have taken that into account when writing the pattern.

Materials

A—9 (10, 13, 14) skeins of Cleo from Muench Yarns (50 g; 62 yds), color 182 (4)

B—7 (8, 9, 11) skeins of Dune from Trendsetter Yarns (50 g; 90 yds), color 76 (5)

C—5 (5, 6, 7) skeins of Merino 8 from Lane Borgosesia (50 g; 137 yds), color 250 (3)

Trim: 1 skein *each* of Dolcino from Trendsetter Yarns (50 g; 100 yds), color 11 Grey and color 103 Tan (4)

Size 11 needles

Size 15 needles or size required to obtain gauge

Size K crochet hook

Gauge

10 sts and 12 rows = 4" in St st with 3 yarns held tog on larger needles

Sleeves

- With smaller needle and 1 strand each of A, B, and C held tog, CO 15 (16, 18, 20) sts. Work 4 rows garter st.

- Change to larger needle and St st and inc 4 sts evenly spaced across—19 (20, 22, 24) sts. Cont to inc 1 st at each edge every 5th row 10 times—39 (40, 42, 44) sts. Work until sleeve measures 15½ (16, 16½, 17)" or desired length to underarm (holding upright when measuring to allow for stretch).

- **Shape cap:** BO 3 sts at beg next 2 rows. Dec 1 st at each edge EOR to cap depth of 4½ (5, 5½, 6)"—sleeve should be approx 20 (21, 22, 23)" from beg. BO 3 sts at beg next 2 rows. BO rem sts.

Back

- With smaller needle and 1 strand each of A, B, and C held tog, CO 54 (62, 66, 74) sts. Work 4 rows garter st, then change to larger needle and St st and dec 1 st at each edge every 4" three times—

48 (56, 60, 68) sts. Inc 1 st at each edge every 2" twice—52 (60, 64, 72) sts. Work to 15½ (16½, 17½, 18½)".

- **Shape armholes:** BO 3 sts at beg next 2 rows. Dec 1 st at each edge EOR 7 times—32 (40, 44, 52) sts. Work even until armhole depth measures 8 (8½, 9, 9½)"—total body length should be 23½ (25, 26½, 28)". BO rem sts.

Left Front

- With smaller needle and 1 strand each of A, B, and C held tog, CO 29 (32, 35, 39) sts. Work 4 rows garter st, then change to larger needle and St st and dec 1 st at beg of RS row, and then every 4" twice—26 (29, 32, 36) sts. Inc 1 st at beg of RS row every 2" twice—28 (31, 34, 38) sts. Work until piece measures 14½ (15½, 16½, 17½)" from beg.

- **Shape neck and armhole:** Dec 1 st at neck edge every 3 rows 8 (8, 9, 9) times, and AT SAME TIME at 15½ (16½, 17½, 18½)", shape armhole as for back. When same length as back, BO all sts.

Right Front

Work as for left front, rev all shaping.

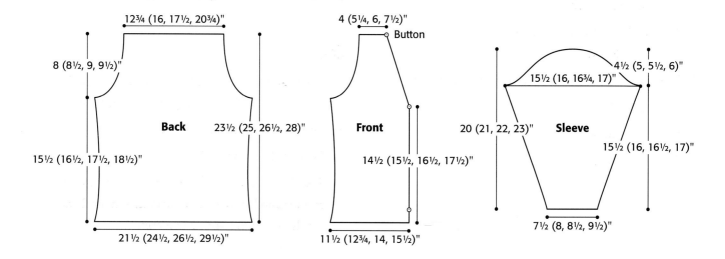

Back — 12¾ (16, 17½, 20¾)" ; 8 (8½, 9, 9½)" ; 23½ (25, 26½, 28)" ; 15½ (16½, 17½, 18½)" ; 21½ (24½, 26½, 29½)"

Front — 4 (5¼, 6, 7½)" Button ; 14½ (15½, 16½, 17½)" ; 11½ (12¾, 14, 15½)"

Sleeve — 4½ (5, 5½, 6)" ; 15½ (16, 16¾, 17)" ; 20 (21, 22, 23)" ; 15½ (16, 16½, 17)" ; 7½ (8, 8½, 9½)"

Finishing

- Sew shoulder, side, and sleeve seams.

- Set sleeves into armhole edges.

- **Edging:** With crochet hook and 1 strand each color Dolcino held tog, work 3 rows sc along front and neck edges, holding garment up often while working first row to make sure that band is not sagging or pulling up too much. Work 1 rnd rsc around entire front, neck, and bottom edges. Work 1 rnd rsc around sleeve bottom edges.

Fake Fur Collar

Lush, furry yarns are worked double strand for extra body. The collar is worked from the center edge out, so be sure to check your gauge. Better to err on the side of a bit short—the yarns are heavy and the collar will easily stretch in length. Increases around the neck area produce a rounded shape for ease of wearing. The collar looks great as a wild scarf, too.

Size

10" deep at widest point, length to match cardigan

Materials

A—4 skeins of Fern from Prism Yarns (2 oz; 45 yds), color Mink (5)

B—2 skeins of Merlyn from Prism Yarns (2 oz; 122 yds), color Mink (4)

Size 13 needles or size required to obtain gauge

Size 15 needles

Size J crochet hook

2 stitch markers

Gauge

10 sts and 20 rows = 4" in garter st with 1 strand each of A and B held tog on larger needle

Collar

- With larger needles and 1 strand each A and B held tog, CO 80 sts. Change to smaller needle.

- **Row 1:** K30, pm, K20, pm, K30.

  Rows 2, 3, and 4: Knit.

  Row 5: Inc in first and last st, inc 1 st after first marker and before second marker, and inc 2 sts evenly spaced between 2 markers.

- BO 4 sts at beg of next 4 rows, and AT SAME TIME inc 1 st at each marker and 2 sts between 2 markers as established. BO 5 sts at beg of next 6 rows. BO 8 sts at beg of next 8 rows. BO rem sts, fasten off.

Finishing

- Place collar over sweater front and neck to check for size. With crochet hook and with 1 strand each of A and B held tog, work 1 rnd sc and 1 rnd rsc around entire collar, making sure that inside is same length as front/neck opening (you may have to crochet a bit tighter than knitting to ease it in) and outside is loose enough to lie flat, especially around shoulders.

- Sew 6 small buttons to inside of cardigan: 1 at each shoulder seam, the beg of neck shaping, and about 2" from bottom edge.

- **Button loops:** With matching sewing thread, make a button loop on inside edge of collar to correspond to buttons as follows: Thread needle with double length of thread. Make a small anchoring tack on collar; then carefully make a loop that is correct size for button. Make a 2nd loop same size; then work buttonhole stitch over double strand.

Collar

Rows 6, 7, and 8: Knit.

Row 9: Inc 1 st in first and last st; inc 1 st after first marker and before second marker, and inc 3 sts evenly spaced between 2 markers.

Rows 10, 11, and 12: Knit.

Row 13: Rep row 9.

Rows 14, 15, and 16: Knit.

Curly Mohair Collar

I found a fantastic skein of handspun Mohair Curls at a Stitches Market expo. Of course I bought it, and it has graced my studio for the last 10 years or so. This yarn was the original inspiration for the cardigan, but I made the fake fur collar first because I had lots of that yarn available. As it turns out, I was wise to do so, because there was just enough of the Moira to finish the collar, and even at that I had to adjust the pattern for larger bind offs and less of a curve. The collar is just as luxurious, though, so making it a bit smaller didn't turn out to be a problem.

Size

7" deep at widest point; length to match cardigan

Materials

1 skein of Moira* from Rosalie Truong (handspun mohair/cotton; 200 yds), color Azleene

Size 15 needles

Skein size is variable; my skein was 14¾ oz and approx 200 yds.

Gauge

10 sts and 20 rows = 4" in garter st

Collar

- Work as for Fake Fur Collar on page 119, up to row 15.

  Row 15: BO 5 sts at beg of next 2 rows and inc at each marker and twice more between markers.

- BO 10 sts at beg next 2 rows. BO 15 sts at beg of next 2 rows and AT SAME TIME on first row of BO, inc 1 st after first marker and before second marker, and inc 2 sts evenly spaced between 2 markers. BO rem sts.

Finishing

Attach buttons and make button loops as for Fake Fur Collar (page 20).

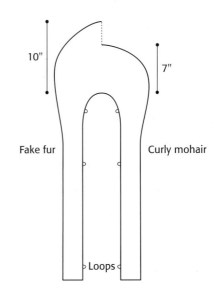

FINISHING UP

When all is said and knit, the pieces must be assembled. I love this part of knitting, because good finishing can correct flaws in both design and fit—those little pesky things that just didn't work out the way we wanted. Good finishing ensures that the sweater sits properly across your shoulders, the sleeve length is perfect, and the sweater fits around the body without pulling. Gently block each piece with steam after knitting. Use an ironing board, a bed, or an out-of-the-way section of carpet covered with a sheet. T-pins will keep the pieces flat and blocked to size while you steam.

Refer to the diagram as a guide for laying out the pieces, wrong side up. With a steamer or good steam iron, gently steam the entire surface, paying particular attention to any edges that might be rolling. Be careful not to put the weight of the iron on the knitting. Allow the pieces to dry; then remove the pins, and the project is ready for seaming.

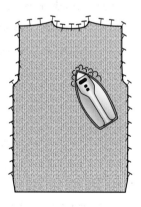

Seaming

I prefer sewing vertical seams with the mattress stitch, which is worked from the right side and provides an invisible seam. Place two pieces to be seamed on a table, right side up and aligned along the edge to be sewn. Begin at the lower edge, either with the long tail from the cast on or with new yarn attached firmly to the selvage. Insert the needle under two horizontal bars between the first and second

stitches from the edge and then under two stitches at the same place on the opposite piece. Pull the yarn firmly in the direction of the open portion of the seam. Be sure to go into the stitch you came out of, and then proceed up, working under two horizontal bars on each side and pulling the seam together as you work.

Pull tight every inch or so.

For shoulder seams, firmly bind off and then invisibly weave the seams together on the right side, which provides an almost invisible seam. By binding off firmly rather than loosely, the shoulder area, which bears the weight of the sweater, becomes stabilized. Place the two pieces on a table, right sides up and shoulders aligned. With attached yarn, insert the needle into the V of the first stitch on the piece nearest you and then through the V of the first stitch on the other piece. Insert the needle through both threads that make the V of the next stitch on the piece nearest you and then through the threads of the same V on the other piece. Pull the tension just enough so that the stitch you have made looks just like the knitting.

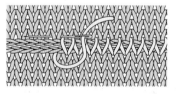

To sew set-in, inset, or drop-shouldered sleeves to the body, use the mattress stitch along the sides of the sleeve cap, and combine the mattress stitch along the body piece with invisible weaving where the cap levels off at the top. Sew the sleeve top or sleeve cap to the body by centering it to the shoulder seam and working down each side separately.

Crochet Edgings

One of my favorite edge finishes is a row of single crochet followed by a row of reverse single crochet (also known as crab stitch). This can be worked successfully on pieces that have little natural roll.

Single Crochet (sc)

Working from right to left with the right side of the work facing you, insert a crochet hook into the first knit stitch, draw up a loop, wrap yarn around the hook, and draw it through the loop on the hook (yarn fastened to knitting); *insert the hook into the next stitch, draw up a loop, wrap the yarn around the hook, and draw through both loops (stitch made)*, repeat from * to *. Stop every few inches and examine the edge. It should be just barely tighter than the knitting, because the row of reverse crochet will spread it out a bit more.

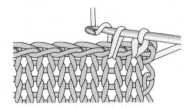

Insert hook into stitch, yarn over hook, pull loop through to front, yarn over hook.

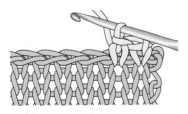

Pull loop through both loops on hook.

TIP: If you have trouble making the edge lie flat when crocheting, try this trick: Work the foundation row of single crochet with the specified hook. Work one stitch in three or four knit stitches, then skip one, both when working across stitches and when working across rows. The single crochet row should pull in just a bit, and the next row will spread it out. For the reverse single crochet row, use a hook that is one size smaller than that used for the foundation.

Reverse Single Crochet (rsc)

This is usually worked on a foundation row of single crochet. Working from left to right, with the right side facing you, insert the hook into the single crochet stitch to the right, draw up a loop, and then wrap and draw through both loops (stitch made). Repeat, moving from left to right. Always keep your hook parallel to the work. If you twist your hand around when inserting the hook, the stitch will be incorrect. Notice that keeping your hook parallel to the work is a bit awkward, but it gets easier as you practice. Keeping the tension a bit looser makes it easier to work.

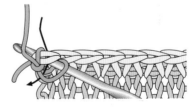

Join yarn with slip stitch. Insert hook into first stitch to the right.

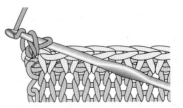

Yarn over hook, pull through both loops on hook, keeping hook parallel to work.

Half Double and Double Crochet

One step further than single crochet, the half double and double crochet can build up edge depth more quickly.

Half double crochet (hdc): Working from right to left with right side of work facing you, *wrap yarn once around hook, insert hook into next stitch, draw up loop, wrap yarn around hook and draw through all 3 loops (stitch made)*; repeat from * to *.

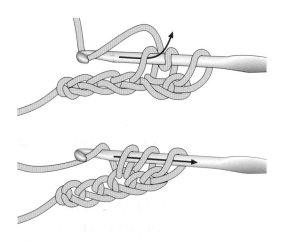

Double crochet (dc): Working from right to left with right side of work facing you ,*wrap yarn around hook, insert hook into next stitch, draw up loop (wrap yarn around hook and draw through 2 loops) twice*, repeat from * to *.

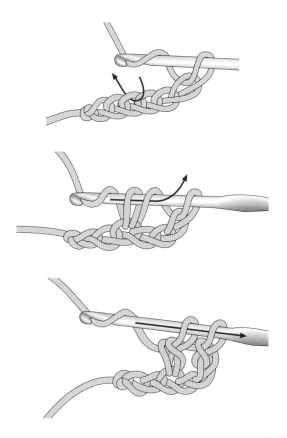

Knitted Bands

The front bands will be one of the last steps in completing a cardigan, and we are fortunate to have a gauge already done: the band at the bottom of the sweater. Hold the finished back up sideways (so the border is in the same direction as it will sit on the front), and while a friend holds the piece this way, take a total measurement of the border from one edge to the other. This mimics how the garment will behave when the same border is on the front.

Divide the measurement by the number of stitches in the border and you have a border gauge. Measure along the front edge of the sweater and multiply this measurement by the border gauge. This is the number of stitches needed for the front band. The same can be done around the neck edge, with the garment lying flat and a flexible tape measure going around the curves. For a V neck, measure to the beginning of the neck (A–B), then again along the neck to the shoulder (B–C), and across the back neck (C–D). Keep the number of stitches to each point separate, to help in picking them up evenly and centered. Use split-ring markers to mark shoulder seams and the beginning of the neck shaping.

With the right side facing you, beginning at the lower-left front corner and with the same needle used for the other borders, pick up as if to knit the stitches evenly spaced along the front edge. Work in the border pattern for the desired width and bind off in pattern. Make sure that the bind off is neither too tight (band will pull up) nor too loose (band will waver and not lie flat.) Measure the left-side band for buttonhole spacing, keeping in mind that if it is a crew neck you will also put a button in the neck band. Make the right-side band, making buttonholes in the middle of the width.

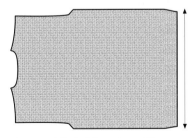

Measure while holding piece sideways.
Divide stitches by measurement = gauge.

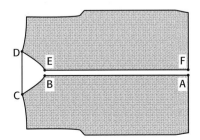

Final finishing should include another session with the steamer. With the garment inside out, gently pat steam onto all seams to flatten them slightly. Pat the neck and front bands, and allow the garment to dry.

Care

Most knitted garments can be gently hand washed in mild detergent and lukewarm water. Yarn labels that say "dry clean only" should be followed, but if a label reads "dry cleaning recommended," gentle hand washing should not harm the fibers. The key to washing any fine textile is to neither shock nor stretch it. Shocking occurs when the water temperature varies by more than a few degrees. Stretching occurs through agitation or by picking up a heavy, wet garment by one part or edge. The wash and rinse waters should be the same temperature, and the entire garment must be supported as it is lifted from the basin. The wet garment can be placed in the washing machine and run through the "spin" cycle to help remove excess water. You can place the garment in a lingerie bag to provide extra protection. Be certain that the washer is set on spin only, with no agitation and no rinse water coming in. Remove the garment and lay it flat on a screen or towel, patting it into shape. Allow to dry. The surface may be brushed gently with a lint brush to raise the nap.

ABBREVIATIONS AND GLOSSARY

approx	approximately
beg	begin(ning)
BO	bind off
CC	contrasting color
CO	cast on
cont	continue
dc	double crochet
dec	decrease
EOR	every other row
garter st	garter stitch; knit every row
hdc	half double crochet
inc	increase
K1f&b	knit into front and then into back of same stitch
K2tog	knit 2 stitches together
kwise	knitwise; as if to knit
MC	main color
patt	pattern
pm	place marker
PU	pick up and knit

rem	remain(ing)
rep(s)	repeat(s)
rnd(s)	round(s)
RS	right side
rsc	reverse single crochet
sc	single crochet
sl st	slip stitch from left to right needle purlwise unless specified otherwise
sm	slip marker
ssk	slip a stitch knitwise, slip another stitch knitwise, knit these 2 stitches together through the back loop
st(s)	stitch(es)
St st	Stockinette stitch; knit on right-side rows, purl on wrong-side rows
tbl	through back loop
tog	together
wyib	with yarn in back
wyif	with yarn in front
WS	wrong side
YO	yarn over

RESOURCES

For a list of shops in your area or for mail order and Internet companies that carry the yarns mentioned in the book, contact the following companies:

Classic Elite Yarns Inc.
122 Western Ave.
Lowell, MA 01851-1434
www.classiceliteyarns.com

Exquisitely Angora/Rosalie Truong
1222 Mackay Pl.
St. Louis, MO 63104
www.angorayarn.com

Himalaya Yarn
149 Mallard Dr.
Colchester, VT 05446
www.himalayayarn.com

Mango Moon
412 N. Coast Hwy #114
Laguna Beach, CA 92651
www.mangomoonyarns.com

Muench Yarns Inc.
1323 Scott St.
Petaluma, CA 94954
www.muenchyarns.com

Pastora the Color Lady
14068 Indian Springs Rd.
Penn Valley, CA 95946
www.pastora.net

Prism Yarns Inc.
3140 39th Ave. N.
St. Petersburg, FL 33714
www.prismyarn.com

Tahki/Stacy Charles Inc.
8000 Cooper Avenue Bldg. 6
Glendale, NY 11385
www.tahkistacycharles.com

Thistle Hill Farm/Kristin Thomas Woolens
RR 1, Box 169
Morrisville, NY 13408

Trendsetter Yarns/Lane Borgosesia
16745 Saticoy St. Suite #101
Van Nuys, CA 91406
www.trendsetteryarns.com

Knitting and Crochet Titles

Martingale & COMPANY

America's Best-Loved Craft & Hobby Books®
America's Best-Loved Knitting Books®

CROCHET

Classic Crocheted Vests

Crochet for Babies and Toddlers

Crochet for Tots

Crochet from the Heart

Crocheted Aran Sweaters

Crocheted Lace

Crocheted Socks!

Crocheted Sweaters

The Essential Book of Crochet Techniques *NEW!*

Eye-Catching Crochet *NEW!*

First Crochet

Fun and Funky Crochet

The Little Box of Crocheted Hats and Scarves

The Little Box of Crocheted Ponchos and Wraps *NEW!*

More Crocheted Aran Sweaters

KNITTING

200 Knitted Blocks

365 Knitting Stitches a Year: Perpetual Calendar

Big Knitting

Blankets, Hats, and Booties *NEW!*

Dazzling Knits

Everyday Style *NEW!*

Fair Isle Sweaters Simplified

First Knits

Funky Chunky Knitted Accessories *NEW!*

Handknit Style

Knits for Children and Their Teddies

Knits from the Heart

Knitted Shawls, Stoles, and Scarves

The Knitter's Book of Finishing Techniques

Knitting with Hand-Dyed Yarns

Knitting with Novelty Yarns

Lavish Lace

The Little Box of Knitted Ponchos and Wraps

The Little Box of Knitted Throws

The Little Box of Scarves

The Little Box of Scarves II

The Little Box of Sweaters

Perfectly Brilliant Knits

The Pleasures of Knitting

Pursenalities

Pursenality Plus *NEW!*

Rainbow Knits for Kids

Ribbon Style *NEW!*

Sarah Dallas Knitting

Saturday Sweaters

Sensational Knitted Socks

Simply Beautiful Sweaters

A Treasury of Rowan Knits

The Ultimate Knitted Tee

The Yarn Stash Workbook *NEW!*

Our books are available at bookstores and your favorite craft, fabric, and yarn retailers. If you don't see the title you're looking for, visit us at **www.martingale-pub.com** or contact us at:

1-800-426-3126

International: 1-425-483-3313
Fax: 1-425-486-7596
Email: info@martingale-pub.com